LEAP REHEARSAL AND SKILLS MASTERY

This Book Includes:

- **Access to Online Practice Assessments**
  - 2 LEAP Practice Tests
  - Self-paced learning and personalized score reports
  - Strategies for building speed and accuracy
  - Instant feedback after completion of the Assessments

- **Standards based practice**
  - Reading: Literature
  - Reading: Informational Text
  - Language

- **Detailed answer explanations for every question**

Complement Classroom Learning All Year

Using the Lumos Study Program, teachers and parents can reinforce the classroom learning experience for children. It creates a collaborative learning platform for students, teachers and Parents.

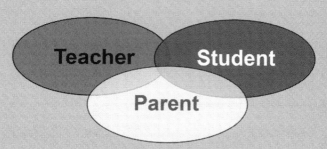

Used in Schools To Improve Student Achievement

Lumos Learning
Developed by Expert Teachers

LEAP Test Prep: Grade 8 English Language Arts Literacy (ELA) Practice Workbook and Full-length Online Assessments: LEAP Study Guide

Contributing Editor   -   **Erin Schollaert**
Contributing Editor   -   **Nina Anderson**
Executive Producer   -   **Mukunda Krishnaswamy**
Designer and Illustrator -   **Harini N.**

COPYRIGHT ©2016 by Lumos Information Services, LLC. **ALL RIGHTS RESERVED**. No part of this work covered by the copyright hereon may be reproduced or used in any form or by an means graphic, electronic, or mechanical, including photocopying, recording, taping, Web distribution or information storage and retrieval systems- without the written permission of the publisher.

NGA Center/CCSSO are the sole owners and developers of the Common Core State Standards, which does not sponsor or endorse this product. © Copyright 2010. National Governors Association Center for Best Practices and Council of Chief State School Officers.

Louisiana Department of Education is not affiliated to Lumos Learning. Louisiana department of education, was not involved in the production of, and does not endorse these products or this site.

ISBN-10: 1-9457-3035-8

ISBN-13: 978-1-9457-3035-1

Printed in the United States of America

For permissions and additional information contact us

Lumos Information Services, LLC
PO Box 1575, Piscataway, NJ 08855-1575
http://www.LumosLearning.com

Email: support@lumoslearning.com
Tel: (732) 384-0146
Fax: (866) 283-6471

Developed by Expert Teachers

Table of Contents

© Lumos Information Services 2016 | LumosLearning.com

Introduction

This book is designed to help students get LEAP Assessment rehearsal along with standards aligned rigorous skills practice. Unlike a traditional book, this Lumos tedBook offers two full-length practice tests online. Taking these tests will not only help students get a comprehensive review of standards assessed on the LEAP, but also become familiar with the technology enhanced question types.

After students take the test online, educators can use the results of the score report to assign specific lessons provided in this book.

Students will obtain a better understanding of each standard and improve on their weaknesses by practicing the content of this workbook. The lessons contain rigorous questions aligned to the state standards and substandards. Taking the time to work through the activities will afford students the ability to become proficient in each grade level standard.

Quick facts about the LEAP Test

- Louisiana Educational Assessment Program (LEAP) is based on Louisiana Student standards which is aligned to the Common Core Standards.
- Required for all students in grades 3-10 in states opting for LEAP assessments.
- Each student will be assessed in English, Reading, Math, Science and Writing
- 3 ½ to 3 ¾ hours total testing time per grade.
- It's a Computer-based test with hardship waivers available for paper/pencil administration.
- LEAP first round of testing occurred during the 2015 – 2016 school year.

English Language Arts Literacy Estimated Time on Task in Minutes			
Grade	Session 1	Session 2	Session 3
3	75	75	60
4	90	75	75
5	90	75	75
6	90	75	75
7	90	75	75
8	90	75	75

How Can the Lumos Study Program Prepare Students for LEAP Tests?

At Lumos Learning, we believe that year-long learning and adequate practice before the actual test are the keys to success on LEAP test. We have designed the Lumos study program to help students get plenty of realistic practice before the test and to promote year-long collaborative learning.

This is a Lumos tedBook™. It connects you to Online LEAP Assessments and additional resources. You can access these resources using a number of devices including personal computers, Android/ iOS phones and tablets. The Lumos StepUp Online Assessment is designed to promote year-long learning. It is a simple program students can securely access using a computer or device with internet access. Students will get instant feedback and can review their answers anytime. Each student's answers and progress can be reviewed by parents and educators to reinforce the learning experience.

© Lumos Information Services 2016 | LumosLearning.com

How to access the Lumos LEAP Online Assessments

 Important Instruction: Please note that Lumos LEAP practice tests are provided in the online format only. Use the instructions provided on this page to access two full-length assessments.

First Time Access:

Using a personal computer with internet access:	Using a smartphone or tablet:
Go to http://www.lumoslearning.com/a/workbooks	Scan the QR Code below and follow the instructions.
Select your State and enter the following access code in the Access Code field and press the 'Submit' button.	
Access Code: LEAPG8E-74512-P	

In the next screen, click on the "Register" button to register your user name and password.

Subsequent Access:

After you establish your user id and password for subsequent access, simply login with your account information.

What if I buy more than one Lumos Study Program?

Please note that you can use all Online Workbooks with one User ID and Password. If you buy more than one book, you will access them with the same account.

Go back to the **http://lumoslearning.com/a/workbooks** link and enter the access code provided in the second book. In the next screen simply login using your previously created account.

How to create a teacher account

- You can use the Lumos online programs along with this book to complement and extend your classroom instruction.

- Get a Teacher account by visiting LumosLearning.com/a/leapg8ela

  This Lumos StepUp® Basic teacher account will help you:

  - Create up to 30 student accounts
  - Review the online work of your students
  - Get insightful student reports
  - Discover standards aligned videos, apps and books through EdSearch
  - Easily access CCSS
  - Create and share information about your classroom or school events

  NOTE: There is a limit of one grade and subject per teacher for the free account.

  Mobile Access to the Teacher Portal: To access your student reports on a mobile device, download the Lumos SchoolUp™ mobile app using the instructions provided in "How can I Download the App?" section of this chapter.

QR code for Teacher account

© Lumos Information Services 2016 | LumosLearning.com

Test Taking Tips

1) **The day before the test,** make sure you get a good night's sleep.

2) **On the day of the test,** be sure to eat a good hearty breakfast! Also, be sure to arrive at school on time.

3) **During the test:**

- **Read every question carefully.**

  - Do not spend too much time on any one question. Work steadily through all questions in the section.
  - Attempt all of the questions even if you are not sure of some answers.
  - If you run into a difficult question, eliminate as many choices as you can and then pick the best one from the remaining choices. Intelligent guessing will help you increase your score.
  - Also, mark the question so that if you have extra time, you can return to it after you reach the end of the section.
  - Some questions may refer to a graph, chart, or other kind of picture. Carefully review the graphic before answering the question.
  - Be sure to include explanations for your written responses and show all work.

- **While Answering Multiple-Choice (EBSR) questions.**

  - EBSR questions come in 2 parts - PART A and B.
  - Both PART A and B could be multiple choice or Part A could be multiple choice while Part B could be some other type.
  - Generally, Part A and B will be related, sometimes it may just be from the same lesson but not related questions.
  - If it is a Multiple choice question, Select the bubble corresponding to your answer choice.
  - Read all of the answer choices, even if think you have found the correct answer.
  - In case the questions in EBSR are not multiple choice questions, follow the instruction for other question types while answering such questions.

- **While Answering TECR questions.**

  - Read the directions of each question. Some might ask you to drag something, others to select, and still others to highlight. Follow all instructions of the question (or questions if it is in multiple parts)

How to use this book effectively

The Lumos Program is a flexible learning tool. It can be adapted to suit a student's skill level and the time available to practice before standardized tests. Here are some tips to help you use this book and the online resources effectively:

Students

- The standards in each book can be practiced in the order designed, or in the order of your own choosing.
- Complete all questions in each workbook.
- Take the first practice assessment online which has three sessions.
- Have open-ended questions evaluated by a teacher or parent, keeping in mind the scoring rubrics.
- Take the second practice assessment as you get close to the official test date. This will also have three sessions.
- Complete the test in a quiet place, following the test guidelines. Practice tests provide you an opportunity to improve your test taking skills and to review topics included in the LEAP test.

Parents

- Familiarize yourself with the LEAP test format and expectations.
- Help your child use Lumos StepUp® LEAP Online Assessments by following the instructions in "How to access the Lumos LEAP Online Assessments" section of this chapter.
- Review your child's performance in the "Lumos LEAP Online Assessments" periodically. You can do this by simply asking your child to log into the system online and selecting the subject area you wish to review.
- Get useful information about your school by downloading the Lumos SchoolUp™ app. Please follow directions provided in "How can I Download the App?" section of this chapter.

© Lumos Information Services 2016 | LumosLearning.com

Reading: Literature
Key Ideas and Details

Lesson 1: Textual Evidence (RL.8.1)

Archaeology is the study of past human life and culture through systematically examining and interpreting the material remains left behind. These material remains include archaeological sites (e.g. settlements, building features, graves), as well as cultural materials or artifacts such as tools and pottery. Through the interpretation and classification of archaeological materials, archaeologists work to understand past human behavior. In some countries, archaeology is often historical or art historical, with a strong emphasis on Culture history, archaeological sites, and artifacts such as art objects. In the New World, archaeology can be either a part of history and classical studies or anthropology.

The exact origins of archaeology as a discipline are uncertain. Excavations of ancient monuments and the collection of antiquities have been taking place for thousands of years. It was only in the 19th century, however, that the systematic study of the past through its physical remains began to be carried out in a manner recognizable to modern students of archaeology.

1.   According to the above passage, what changed in the 19th century?

    Ⓐ The study of archaeology became more accessible to modern students.

    Ⓑ The techniques used for study were more systematic and understandable for modern students.

    Ⓒ The study of archaeology and anthropology were tied together.

    Ⓓ The interpretation and classification of archaeological materials changed.

Sympathy

I lay in sorrow, deep distressed;
My grief a proud man heard;
His looks were cold, he gave me gold,
But not a kindly word.

My sorrow passed-I paid him back
The gold he gave to me;
Then stood erect and spoke my thanks
And blessed his charity.

I lay in want, and grief, and pain;
A poor man passed my way;
He bound my head, He gave me bread,
He watched me day and night.

How shall I pay him back again
For all he did to me ?
Oh, gold is great, but greater far
Is heavenly sympathy.

- 　　　Charles Mackay

2.　According to the poet, what did he feel was most important?

Ⓐ giving away food
Ⓑ blessing charity
Ⓒ sympathy
Ⓓ gold

3.　What does the first stanza tell us about the poet?

Ⓐ The poet experienced an event which made him deeply sorrowful.
Ⓑ The poet wrote this poem when he was a proud man.
Ⓒ The poet wrote this poem when he was in need of money.
Ⓓ The poet was friends with the proud man.

© Lumos Information Services 2016 | LumosLearning.com

Stephen and Joseph Montgolfier were papermakers, but they had been interested in flying for many years. One night, in 1782, Joseph noticed something that gave him an idea. He was sitting in front of the fire when he saw some small pieces of scorched paper being carried up the chimney.

Soon afterward, the brothers conducted an experiment. They lit a fire under a small silk bag, which was open at the bottom; at once, the bag rose to the ceiling. After this, Stephen and Joseph conducted many more experiments, both indoors and in the open air. Eventually, they built a huge balloon of linen and paper. On June 5th, 1783, they launched their balloon in the village of Annonay.

4. **Which sentence in this article tells the reader that the Montgolfier brothers should receive credit for the discovery of the hot air balloon?**

   Ⓐ He was sitting in front of the fire when he saw some small pieces of scorched paper being carried up the chimney.

   Ⓑ They lit a fire under a small silk bag, which was open at the bottom; at once, the bag rose to the ceiling.

   Ⓒ Stephen and Joseph Montgolfier were papermakers, but they had been interested in flying for many years.

   Ⓓ Eventually, they built a huge balloon of linen and paper. On June 5th, 1783, they launched this hot air balloon in their village of Annonay.

5. **Which sentence in this article provides text evidence for the inference that the Montgolfier brothers used hot air to lift their balloon?**

   Ⓐ Eventually, they built a huge balloon of linen and paper.

   Ⓑ They lit a fire under a small silk bag, which was open at the bottom; at once the bag rose to the ceiling.

   Ⓒ On June 5th, 1783, they launched their balloon in the village of Annonay.

   Ⓓ One night, in 1782, Joseph noticed something that gave him an idea.

6. **What evidence from the text can allow readers to infer that Joseph Montgolfier was very observant?**

   Ⓐ He created a balloon from paper and linen.

   Ⓑ He noticed the small pieces of burnt paper being carried up the chimney.

   Ⓒ He found the best location to launch the balloon.

   Ⓓ He was interested in flying.

Megan couldn't believe her luck. She had been standing in line with her best friend Jessica for thirty minutes. Their excitement was mounting as they neared the front of the line for the famed Greased Lightning rollercoaster. Just as they took their seats, the clouds opened up. Soaking wet and disappointed, the girls followed the directions of the ride employees and took shelter under the nearby canopies.

7.   What happened as Megan and Jessica boarded the ride?

Ⓐ It started to rain and they had to find shelter.

Ⓑ The park closed so they had to leave.

Ⓒ One of them spilled soda on the other and they both got wet.

Ⓓ They became overheated and had to find some shade.

The Lake of Innisfree

I will arise and go now, and go to Innisfree,
And a small cabin build there, of clay and wattles made;
Nine bean-rows will I have there, a hive for the honey-bee,
And live alone in the bee-loud glade.

And I shall have some peace there, for peace comes dropping slow,
Dropping from the veils of the morning to where the cricket sings;
There midnight's all a glimmer, and noon a purple glow,
And evening full of the linnet's wings.

I will arise and go now, for always night and day
I hear lake water lapping with low sounds by the shore;
While I stand on the roadway, or on the pavements grey,
I hear it in the deep heart's core.

-     WB Yeats

About the poet:

William Butler Yeats was an Irish poet and a dramatist. He was one of the foremost figures of 20th century literature and was the driving force behind the Irish literary revival. Together with Lady Gregory and Edward Martin, Yeats founded the Abbey Theater. He served as its chief during its early years and was a pillar of the Irish literary establishment in his later years.

The above well-known poem explores the poet's longing for the peace and tranquility of Innisfree, a place where he spent a lot of time as a boy. This poem is a lyric.

8. **After reading the poem what can you say the poet is yearning for?**

    Ⓐ the lake water and the sound it makes
    Ⓑ the beehive and sound of the bees
    Ⓒ the peace and tranquility of Innisfree
    Ⓓ the vision of midnight's glimmer

9. **According to the poem what do you think the age of the author is?**

    Ⓐ He is old and ready to retire.
    Ⓑ He is a very young boy.
    Ⓒ He is in his mid-thirties.
    Ⓓ He is a baby.

It had been a year since Lauren had seen Bailey. Bailey's family had moved to Qatar leaving Lauren to face the world without her best friend. Anxiously, Lauren waited at the arrival gate hoping to glimpse a peek at her childhood friend. She knew after eleven hours in the air, Bailey would be exhausted; but, she could hardly wait to catch up. Moments later, the doors to the gate flung open, and there was her best friends Bailey.

Once home, the hours passed like minutes as the girls laughed and giggled sharing moments from the last year. It felt as if they had never been apart. But Lauren felt like Bailey was holding something back.

10. **What can you conclude about Bailey?**

    Ⓐ Bailey was moving home.
    Ⓑ Bailey had a secret she wasn't sharing.
    Ⓒ Bailey loved her new home in Qatar.
    Ⓓ None of the above

Lesson 2: Inferences (RL.8.1)

Patrick couldn't believe it. The most important day of his life so far; the day he had been waiting for had finally arrived! He was so excited to show the coaches how hard he had been working on his pitching. He just knew he would make the team this year. Looking at the clock, Patrick realized he was running late. "Bye, Mom," he yelled as he scrambled out of the house. Backing down the driveway, he saw his mom run out of the house, and it looked like she was trying to get his attention. He didn't have time to wait, so he drove off.

Although the school was only five minutes away, the drive felt like an eternity. Two red lights later, Patrick screeched into the parking lot, slammed the car into park, and ran around to the trunk to get his bat bag. It wasn't there. Every piece of equipment he needed to prove himself to the coaches this year was in that bag.

1.   What was Patrick's mom likely trying to tell Patrick?

   Ⓐ   "Don't drive too fast!"
   Ⓑ   "Don't be late for tryouts!"
   Ⓒ   "Be careful driving!"
   Ⓓ   He forgot his bat bag!

2.   What can the reader infer about Patrick after reading the story?

   Ⓐ   He had tried out for the team before and not made it.
   Ⓑ   He was a fast runner.
   Ⓒ   He was not at all ready for tryouts.
   Ⓓ   He was not excited to tryout for the team.

Elizabeth had done it again. She was in such a hurry; she didn't check to make sure she had everything she needed for the drive to work. Just as she slammed the door behind her, she realized, too late, that she wasn't going anywhere fast.

3.   What did Elizabeth forget?

   Ⓐ   her running shoes
   Ⓑ   her keys
   Ⓒ   her briefcase
   Ⓓ   her workout cloths

When Samantha saw the new boy in class, her heart started pounding so fast and loudly that she was certain everybody could hear it. She straightened her posture and gently swept her bangs behind her right ear. As the boy sat down next to her, she gave him a quick glance and then a friendly smile. She was sure he noticed her bright red cheeks as she bent over her paper.

4.   Which of the following can be inferred about Samantha based on the above passage?

- Ⓐ She thought the boy had a nice backpack.
- Ⓑ She was scared of the boy.
- Ⓒ She thought the boy was cute.
- Ⓓ She thought the boy was mean.

Maya and her family were headed to the beach one sunny, summer afternoon. When they arrived, Maya noticed a family seemed to be having what appeared to be garage sale, which was a curious sight to see in the beach parking lot. They were selling used personal items that you would normally find in one's house like pots, pans, dishes, a CD player, and various other items. There appeared to be a mother, father, and two children, a boy and a girl about Maya's age. Maya could tell that the family was not there to enjoy the beach as they were not dressed for the beach. Their clothes were far too warm for the beautiful day and were tattered, torn and quite dingy. Suddenly, Maya remembered that she had a twenty dollar bill in her pocket that she had received for her birthday.

5.   Based on the information in the passage, infer what you think will happen next.

- Ⓐ Maya will buy something from the family's garage sale.
- Ⓑ Maya will want to buy something, but she already has all of those items in her house, so she won't buy anything.
- Ⓒ Maya will give the money to her family.
- Ⓓ Maya will use the money for snacks for the family.

Haley was putting the finishing touches on her famous apple pie when the phone rang. She dashed to answer it. After all, this might be the call that she had been waiting for. Even though her hands were still covered in flour, she grabbed the phone before it could ring a second time.

"Hello. You've reached the Williams residence," she said, trying to make her voice sound calm and collected.

"Is this Haley Williams?" asked the voice on the other end of the line.

"Yes, it is. How may I help you?" Haley replied.

"Ms. Haley Williams, we are proud to announce that you are a finalist in the National Pie Competition. The championship round will be held next weekend in Tampa, Florida. You and your family are invited to join us. Good luck!"

"Why thank you very much," Haley said graciously. "I am looking forward to it." After hanging up, Haley took a deep breath and let out an ear-piercing scream of excitement. She jumped up and down and ran around the kitchen with glee. In the pandemonium, her apple pie was knocked off the counter and landed on the floor, where her two puppies immediately began to gobble it down. Haley just laughed at the mess. As she cleaned the floor she began to think very carefully about her plan for the upcoming week

With the big competition only one week away, Haley decided that she better make three pies every day. This practice would allow her to experiment with the crust , the filling, and the baking time. She wanted to do everything she possibly could to ensure that her pie was a winner.

Her friend, Max, who was thrilled to find out that Haley was a finalist, offered his kitchen for practice. Haley thanked him. She knew that cooking in an unfamiliar kitchen would be excellent practice for the competition.

Haley worked hard all week, doing nothing but baking pies. Not every pie turned out well. Some had a soggy crust or burned a little on the top. Haley threw out the bad pies and carefully wrapped the successful pies and delivered them to her neighbors and friends. They were all delighted by the surprise and wished Haley good luck at the competition.

The day before the competition, Haley packed up all of the things she would need. She brought her favorite rolling pin for good luck. When she arrived in Tampa, Florida, she went straight to her hotel and got a good night's rest. The competition started early the next morning, and Haley wanted to be ready.

The day of the competition seemed to fly by in one big blur. Haley was one of twelve finalists. Each finalist had their own counter top on which to prepare their pie and their own oven in which to bake it. Once everyone was set up at their station, the master of ceremonies officially started the clock, and everyone got to work. Every contestant had 90 minutes to prepare and bake their pies. Haley mixed and rolled out her pie dough. Then she peeled and sliced her apples, laying them carefully inside the crust. She seasoned the pie with cinnamon and sugar and laid strips of dough on top. She brushed the pie crust with butter and glanced at the clock. She was right on schedule; her pie took 45 minutes to bake and there were just 47 minutes left on the clock.

Haley opened the oven door, but she immediately noticed that something was wrong.

She didn't feel a rush of dry heat in her face, and she realized that she had forgotten to preheat the oven. The oven wasn't hot, and it would take several minutes to reach the correct temperature.

Haley felt her heart sink into her stomach. How could she forget such an important step? In all her practice, she had never forgotten to preheat the oven. Haley figured that she didn't stand a chance of winning, but she refused to give up. She put her pie in the oven and set the oven to the correct temperature.

With 30 seconds left in the competition, Haley removed her pie from the oven. It wasn't golden on the top, but it looked like it was cooked through. Haley sighed, disappointed that she had blown her chances at winning. But she delivered her pie to the judges and hoped for the best.

After tasting each pie and deliberating for hours, the judges handed the results to the master of ceremonies. "In third place....Haley Williams!" the voice boomed over the loud speaker. Haley couldn't believe her ears. She walked to the front of the room to accept her trophy with a smile on her face. She knew that if it hadn't been for her mistake, she might have won the grand prize.

But, she just hugged her trophy, congratulated herself on her accomplishment, and promised herself that she would do better next year.

6.   What can be inferred from Haley's reaction to the phone ringing?

   Ⓐ   She isn't concerned about the phone call.
   Ⓑ   She doesn't think washing her hands is important.
   Ⓒ   She is expecting an important phone call.
   Ⓓ   She is enjoying talking to her family.

Henry sat eagerly in the waiting area of the airport. Over the last year, he'd been putting away a little money each month into what he called his "vacation fund." He bought travel books and researched all of the sites he wanted to see. Now all he had to do was wait until his flight was called.

7.   What can you infer about Henry's trip?

    Ⓐ   It was a spur of the moment idea.

    Ⓑ   It is something he has looked forward to for a long time.

    Ⓒ   It is to a place he's been before.

    Ⓓ   It is to an exotic location.

She pulled hard at the doorknob. The door was difficult to budge. Finally inside, she brushed aside the cobwebs, leaving footprints in the dust on the floor.

8.   What can be inferred from this description?

    Ⓐ   The place she is entering hasn't been used in a long time.

    Ⓑ   The house she is entering is a new structure.

    Ⓒ   The door was locked.

    Ⓓ   She has just bought the house and is preparing to move in.

Justin had Mark's deep brown eyes and his button nose. At only three years old, he already showed signs of Mark's sense of humor and optimism. Mark was proud that Justin had inherited some of his traits.

9.   Based on the description above, what can be inferred about Justin?

    Ⓐ   He is friends with Mark.

    Ⓑ   He is Mark's brother.

    Ⓒ   He is Mark's son.

    Ⓓ   He is Mark's sister.

© Lumos Information Services 2016 | LumosLearning.com

When Melody's mom came home and discovered the vase in pieces on the counter, she said nothing; instead she pursed her lips, put her hand on her left hip and glared at Melody.

10. What can the reader infer about Melody's mom?

- Ⓐ Melody's mom is mad at Melody for breaking the vase. She is waiting for an explanation.
- Ⓑ Melody's mom had a long day at work and just needs a moment to think.
- Ⓒ Melody's mom cannot talk due to some dental work she had done earlier in the day.
- Ⓓ Melody's mom is surprised that her kitchen is so clean.

Lesson 3: Theme (RL.8.2)

1. **What is the difference between a theme and a main idea?**

    (A) A theme is the message of a story, and the main idea what the story is mainly about.
    (B) A theme is a summary, and the main idea is a paraphrase.
    (C) A theme tells what the symbols mean, and the main idea is a symbol.
    (D) A theme is what a student writes, and a main idea is what the story is mainly about.

2. **What is a universal theme?**

    (A) a story that takes place in outer space
    (B) a theme that is implied
    (C) a common theme that could apply to anyone, anywhere, anytime
    (D) a theme that includes an adventure across the universe

Excerpt from *Alice's Adventures in Wonderland* by Lewis Carroll

Alice was beginning to get very tired of sitting by her sister on the bank, and of having nothing to do: once or twice she had peeped into the book her sister was reading, but it had no pictures or conversations in it, 'and what is the use of a book,' thought Alice 'without pictures or conversations?'

So she was considering in her own mind (as well as she could, for the hot day made her feel very sleepy and stupid), whether the pleasure of making a daisy-chain would be worth the trouble of getting up and picking the daisies, when suddenly a White Rabbit with pink eyes ran close by her.

3. **What can you infer about Alice's opinion of reading books?**

    (A) Alice only enjoys reading books when she is learning something.
    (B) Alice lives to spend her free time reading as many books as possible.
    (C) Alice wants nothing to do with books at all.
    (D) Alice occasionally enjoys reading fiction books.

© Lumos Information Services 2016 | LumosLearning.com

4. **What is the best way to find a theme in a story?**

    Ⓐ look at the first sentence of the story.
    Ⓑ look at the names of the characters in a story.
    Ⓒ look at the details in the story to find a larger meaning.
    Ⓓ look at reviews of the story.

5. **What is an implied theme?**

    Ⓐ a theme that is straightforward and requires no guessing
    Ⓑ a theme that is indirectly stated through characters, plot, and setting of a story
    Ⓒ a theme that is common throughout many stories that are told across many different cultures
    Ⓓ a theme that is clearly stated by the main character in the story

The Fox and the Cat

An Aesop's Fable

A Fox was boasting to a Cat of its clever devices for escaping its enemies.

"I have a whole bag of tricks," he said, "which contains a hundred ways of escaping my enemies."

"I have only one," said the Cat; "but I can generally manage with that."

Just at that moment they heard the cry of a pack of hounds coming towards them, and the Cat immediately scampered up a tree and hid herself in the boughs.

"This is my plan," said the Cat. "What are you going to do?"

The Fox thought first of one way, then of another, and while he was debating the hounds came nearer and nearer, and at last the Fox in his confusion was caught up by the hounds and soon killed by the huntsmen. The Cat, who had been looking on, said, "Better one safe way than a hundred on which you cannot reckon."

6. **What is the theme of this story?**

    Ⓐ It is good to make friends with strangers.
    Ⓑ It is better to be a cat than a fox.
    Ⓒ Having one solid plan is better than having many possible ones.
    Ⓓ Foxes are not as smart as cats.

The Ungrateful Son

by Jacob and Wilhelm Grimm

Once, a man was sitting with his wife before their front door. They had a roasted chicken which they were about to eat together. Then the man saw that his aged father was approaching, and he hastily took the chicken and hid it, for he did not want to share it with him. The old man came, had a drink, and went away. Now the son wanted to put the roasted chicken back onto the table, but when he reached for it, it had turned into a large toad, which jumped into his face and sat there and never went away again. If anyone tried to remove it, it looked venomously at him as though it would jump into his face, so that no one dared to touch it. And the ungrateful son was forced to feed the toad every day, or else it would eat from his face. And thus he went to and fro in the world without rest.

7.   What is the theme of this story?

    Ⓐ The theme of the story is to always share what you have to share.

    Ⓑ The theme of the story is to not be afraid of toads because they can keep you from saving someone's life.

    Ⓒ The theme of the story is that you should always feed yourself first, and then you will be strong enough to help others.

    Ⓓ The theme of the story is that you should always share your chicken with your parents.

8.   Why is the theme of "The Ungrateful Son" an implied theme?

    Ⓐ It is indirectly stated, and the reader has to determine the theme through the actions of the characters.

    Ⓑ It is explicitly stated and the reader does not have to guess at all.

    Ⓒ It is obvious and doesn't require much thought.

    Ⓓ none of the above

The Fox and the Crow

Aesop's Fable

A Fox once saw a Crow fly off with a piece of cheese in its beak and settle on a branch of a tree. "That's for me, as I am a Fox," said Master Reynard, and he walked up to the foot of the tree. "Good-day, Mistress Crow," he cried. "How well you are looking today: how glossy your feathers; how bright your eye. I feel sure your voice must surpass that of other birds, just as your figure does; let me hear but one song from you that I may greet you as the Queen of Birds." The Crow lifted up her head and began to caw her best, but the moment she opened her mouth the piece of cheese fell to the ground, only to be snapped up by Master Fox. "That will do," said he. "That was all I wanted. In exchange for your cheese I will give you a piece of advice for the future."

9.   What is the theme of this story?

Ⓐ   Help out your friends.

Ⓑ   Don't trust flatterers.

Ⓒ   Sometimes, a song is necessary.

Ⓓ   You should never have to work for food.

Walk-A-Thon

It was clear there weren't enough funds for the 8th-grade graduation ceremony at the end of the year. Big deal – why should I care? I was on the student council, but I never cared about graduation ceremonies.

It costs about $5,000.00 for the rent, equipment, the insurance and all the other incidentals that pile up when planning a large event. Principal Dorsey told us that he didn't have the money this year. He said that if we wanted to keep the graduation tradition going, we would have to raise the money ourselves. "I'm sure we can live without the ceremony, but it would be nice to have," he told us. Then he left the meeting.

Immediately, Katrina Reynolds shot her hand in the air. She's not very popular, and I always feel kind of sorry for her. "We have to do this, you guys," Katrina gushed. "There is no way we are going to be the only class ever not to have a graduation ceremony."

Then, of course, Abbie Morelle, who was President, shot her hand in the air. I'd been on Student Council for two years, and as far as I could remember, Abbie had never let Katrina say anything without disagreeing with it. "It's very late in the year," Abbie said. "And we already have the Band Land Dance scheduled, which we don't have enough money for. We can't raise $7,000 in, like, two months."

Paulie Roman, who was treasurer, said, "According to my records it would be more like $7,012, although we can't be certain of the precise cost of unspecified expenses related to the ceremony."

I didn't care. To me, 8th grade is pure misery, no matter what you do. If you have a great graduation ceremony at the end of it, that's like saying, "We had such a great time in all of our boring classes and with all of the bullies every day. Let's have a party to celebrate them!" But I was all for a fundraiser if it would get Abbie Morelle off Katrina's back.

I said, "Let's do a walk-a-thon. We could raise a lot of money that way."

"Walk-a-thons are stupid," Abbie said.

Paulie Roman asked, "How much money could we raise with a walk-a-thon?"

I said, "When we did a walk-a-thon for cancer research in elementary school, we raised $4,000. This school is twice as big, and people can walk farther."

"Yeah," Abbie said, "but that was for cancer. Why would anyone give us money for a graduation ceremony? Plus, someone has to organize it, and it's complicated."

That got me mad enough that I had to say, "It's not that complicated. I'll do it."

What was I thinking? I spent the next month doing almost nothing except organizing that walk-a-thon. I hate walk-a-thons, and I hate talking to people about money. I ended up doing way more than I ever wanted to.

Within the first two weeks, I could see that we weren't going to get enough. It was because we weren't raising money for something important, like cancer. So I started telling people that the money would also go for cancer research. Then, when I saw how many people were ready to give more, I just told them it was all for cancer research. I got hundreds of parents signed up, and I got businesses to donate food and decorations.

Abbie was completely jealous.

The walk-a-thon was almost a success, too. But the day before, Principal Dorsey called me into his office. He wanted to know if it was true that I had been telling people that the money would go to cancer research because he had understood the money was going or our 8th-grade graduation party. I didn't answer. He said that he was going to call some of the people who pledged money to ask them if I had said anything about cancer.

"It was the only way I could raise enough money!" I answered back, knowing the lie had caught up with me.

"Well, it was the wrong thing to do." Principal Dorsey replied. "Now, you are going to have to contact every person who donated and let them know the truth. You also may not have enough money for a graduation party now."

I knew I should never have volunteered to lead this.

10.   What is the theme of this story?

    Ⓐ   Don't volunteer to do things.

    Ⓑ   Principals can be very stern.

    Ⓒ   Make sure your intentions are pure, or the results will be disastrous.

    Ⓓ   Walk-a-thons are not the best money-makers.

Lesson 4: Objective Summary (RL.8.2)

1.   **What is an objective summary?**

    (A)   a restatement of the main idea of a text with the addition of the writer's opinion on the idea

    (B)   a restatement of the main idea of a text without the addition of the writer's opinion of the idea

    (C)   a paraphrase of the text with a focus on the writer's opinion and how it affects the main idea of the passage

    (D)   a paraphrase of the text with a focus on the reader's opinion

2.   **An objective summary should** _include both main points and supporting details._

    (A)   include supporting details

    (B)   be brief, accurate, and objective

    (C)   include both main points and supporting details

    (D)   include the reader's opinion of the text

3.   **An objective summary should always** _Show your opinions._

    (A)   clearly show your opinions of the text

    (B)   clearly communicate a summary of the text

    (C)   clearly indicate all the characters in the text

    (D)   include at least four sentences

It had been a year since Lauren had seen Bailey. Bailey's family had moved to Qatar leaving Lauren to face the world without her best friend. Anxiously, Lauren waited at the arrival gate hoping to glimpse a peek at her childhood friend. She knew after eleven hours in the air, Bailey would be exhausted; but, she could hardly wait to catch up. Moments later, the doors to the gate flung open, and there was her best friend, Bailey.

Once home, the hours passed like minutes as the girls laughed and giggled sharing moments from the last year. It felt as if they had never been apart. But Lauren felt like Bailey was holding something back.

4.   What is the best summary for this passage?

(A)   After a year abroad, Lauren was excited about seeing her best friend and catching up.

(B)   Lauren was too excited about seeing her best friend Bailey, and even though she knew Bailey was tired from her flight, she probably talked her ear off.

(C)   Bailey had been gone a year.

(D)   Bailey was Lauren's best friend and though she had been gone a year, she really didn't wasnt to come back.

The Ungrateful Son

by Jacob and Wilhelm Grimm

Once, a man was sitting with his wife before their front door. They had a roasted chicken which they were about to eat together. Then the man saw that his aged father was approaching, and he hastily took the chicken and hid it, for he did not want to share it with him. The old man came, had a drink, and went away. Now the son wanted to put the roasted chicken back onto the table, but when he reached for it, it had turned into a large toad, which jumped into his face and sat there and never went away again. If anyone tried to remove it, it looked venomously at him as though it would jump into his face, so that no one dared to touch it. And the ungrateful son was forced to feed the toad every day, or else it would eat from his face. And thus he went to and fro in the world without rest.

5.   What is the best summary for the story?

(A)   The chicken turned into a toad, and nobody wanted to help the man.

(B)   A man hid his dinner from his father so he didn't have to share it. Because the man was greedy, the chicken turned into a toad, and he was forced to care for it for the rest of his life.

(C)   The man did not like his father. Nobody wanted to help the man get the toad off of his face.

(D)   The man was stuck with a toad on his face for the rest of his life.

The Gettysburg Address

by Abraham Lincoln

Gettysburg, Pennsylvania

November 19, 1863

Four score and seven years ago our fathers brought forth on this continent, a new nation, conceived in Liberty, and dedicated to the proposition that all men are created equal.

Now we are engaged in a great civil war, testing whether that nation, or any nation so conceived and so dedicated, can long endure. We are met on a great battle-field of that war. We have come to dedicate a portion of that field, as a final resting place for those who here gave their lives that nation might live. It is altogether fitting and proper that we should do this.

But, in a larger sense, we can not dedicate – we can not consecrate – we can not hallow – this ground. The brave men, living and dead, who struggled here, have consecrated it, far above our poor power to add or detract. The world will little note, nor long remember what we say here, but it can never forget what they did here. It is for us the living, rather, to be dedicated here to the unfinished work which they who fought here have thus far so nobly advanced. It is rather for us to be here dedicated to the great task remaining before us -- that from these honored dead we take increased devotion to that cause for which they gave the last full measure of devotion -- that we here highly resolve that these dead shall not have died in vain -- that this nation, under God, shall have a new birth of freedom -- and that government of the people, by the people, for the people, shall not perish from the earth.

6. **Which of the following best summarizes President Lincoln's "The Gettysburg Address"?**

Ⓐ In 1863, President Lincoln gave a speech in which he said, "Four score and seven years ago, our fathers brought forth upon this continent a new nation: conceived in liberty, and dedicated to the proposition that all men are created equal. Now we are engaged in a great civil war ... testing whether that nation, or any nation so conceived and so dedicated ... can long endure. We are met on a great battlefield of that war."

Ⓑ In 1863, Abraham Lincoln gave "The Gettysburg Address" which honored those who died fighting in the war and reminded citizens that the soldiers sacrificed their lives for the sake of a democratic government.

Ⓒ A long time ago, President Lincoln gave a speech during the American Civil War about the soldiers who were dying in the war.

Ⓓ In 1863, Abraham Lincoln gave a really boring and complicated speech called "The Gettysburg Address" which honored those who died fighting in the war and reminded citizens that the soldiers sacrificed their lives for the sake of a democratic government.

© Lumos Information Services 2016 | LumosLearning.com

7.   After reading the excerpt from President Lincoln's, "The Gettysburg Address," decide why the following cannot be considered an objective summary.

In 1863, President Lincoln gave a speech, in which it seemed like he was very stressed about the civil war that was taking place in the United States. He thought that equality and freedom that the country was founded on was in jeopardy and that American's were taking these things for granted.

Ⓐ   It is not copied word for word.

Ⓑ   It can be considered an objective summary.

Ⓒ   It does not simply state the facts.

Ⓓ   It does not have enough opinions

From Chapter 5 of **Peter Pan** by J.M. Barrie

"He lay at his ease in a rough chariot drawn and propelled by his men, and instead of a right hand he had the iron hook with which ever and anon he encouraged them to increase their pace. As dogs this terrible man treated and addressed them, and as dogs they obeyed him. In person he was cadaverous [dead looking] and [dark faced], and his hair was dressed in long curls, which at a little distance looked like black candles, and gave a singularly threatening expression to his handsome countenance. His eyes were of the blue of the forget-me-not, and of a profound melancholy, save when he was plunging his hook into you, at which time two red spots appeared in them and lit them up horribly. A man of indomitable courage, it was said that the only thing he shied at was the sight of his own blood, which was thick and of an unusual color. But undoubtedly the grimmest part of him was his iron claw."

8.   Which choice best summarizes the personality of the character in the following excerpt?

Ⓐ   James Hook was a scary man because he had the face of a dead person and had dark curly hair and a hook for his right hand. He treated his men like dogs, and they obeyed him as such. When he was angry, his eyes turned from blue to red.

Ⓑ   James Hook used his appearance to assert his authority in ways that forced others into doing what he wanted. He spoke to and treated his men like dogs, and they were forced to listen. Only the sight of his own blood could waver his courage.

Ⓒ   James Hook was a scary man.

Ⓓ   James Hook was a scary man. James Hook used his appearance to assert his authority in ways that forced others into doing what he wanted. He spoke to and treated his men like dogs, and they were forced to listen. Only the sight of his own blood could waver his courage.

The Emperor Penguin is the only penguin species that breeds during the Antarctic winter. It treks 31–75 miles over the ice to breeding colonies, which may include thousands of penguins. The female lays a single egg, which is then incubated by the male while the female returns to the sea to feed; parents subsequently take turns foraging at sea and caring for their chick in the colony. The average lifespan of the Empire Penguin is 20 years, although observations suggest that some Emperor Penguins may live to 50 years of age.

9.   Read the summary below. Select the answer below that best explains why the summary provided cannot be considered a proper objective summary.

Breeding during the winter in Antarctica is specific to the Emperor Penguin. The Emperor Penguin travels far; they will travel anywhere from 31 – 75 miles in the freezing cold to meet many other penguins for breeding. This is known as a breeding colony and a colony can have thousands of penguins. The father penguins sit on the eggs while the mothers go and hunt for food at sea. After the chick is born, the mother and father take turns taking care of the baby and going off to feed. Emperor Penguins, on average, live to be about 20 years old, but some have been known to live up to 50 years.

    Ⓐ   The summary is incorrect because it includes the writer's opinion.

    Ⓑ   The summary is perfect and should be considered proper.

    Ⓒ   The summary is incorrect because it is not a summary; it is a paraphrase of the passage.

    Ⓓ   The summary is incorrect because it is not accurate.

Walk-A-Thon

It was clear there weren't enough funds for the 8th grade graduation ceremony at the end of the year. Big deal – why should I care? I was on the Student Council, but I never cared about graduation ceremonies.

It costs about $5,000.00 for the rent, equipment, the insurance and all the other incidentals that pile up when planning a large event. Principal Dorsey told us that he didn't have the money this year. He said that if we wanted to keep the graduation tradition going, we would have to raise the money ourselves. "I'm sure we can live without the ceremony, but it would be nice to have," he told us. Then he left the meeting.

Immediately, Katrina Reynolds shot her hand in the air. She's not very popular and I always feel kind of sorry for her. "We have to do this, you guys," Katrina gushed. "There is no way we are going to be the only class ever not to have a graduation ceremony."

Then, of course, Abbie Morelle, who was President, shot her hand in the air. I'd been on Student Council for two years and as far as I could remember, Abbie had never let Katrina say anything without disagreeing with it. "It's very late in the year," Abbie said. "And we already have the Band Land Dance scheduled, which we don't have enough money for. We can't raise $7,000 in, like, two months."

Paulie Roman, who was treasurer, said, "According to my records it would be more like $7,012, although we can't be certain of the precise cost of unspecified expenses related to the ceremony."

I didn't care. To me, 8th grade is pure misery, no matter what you do. If you have a great graduation ceremony at the end of it, that's like saying, "We had such a great time in all of our boring classes, and with all of the bullies every day. Let's have a party to celebrate them!" But I was all for a fundraiser if it would get Abbie Morelle off Katrina's back.

I said, "Let's do a walk-a-thon. We could raise a lot of money that way."

"Walk-a-thons are stupid," Abbie said.

Paulie Roman asked, "How much money could we raise with a walk-a-thon?"

I said, "When we did a walk-a-thon for cancer research in elementary school, we raised $4,000. This school is twice as big and people can walk farther."

"Yeah," Abbie said, "but that was for cancer. Why would anyone give us money for a graduation ceremony? Plus, someone has to organize it, and it's complicated."

That got me mad enough that I had to say, "It's not that complicated. I'll do it."

What was I thinking? I spent the next month doing almost nothing except organizing that walk-a-thon. I hate walk-a-thons, and I hate talking to people about money. I ended up doing way more than I ever wanted to.

Within the first two weeks I could see that we weren't going to get enough. It was because we weren't raising money for something important, like cancer. So I started telling people that the money would also go for cancer research. Then, when I saw how many people were ready to give more, I just told them it was all for cancer research. I got hundreds of parents signed up, and I got businesses to donate food and decorations.

Abbie was completely jealous.

The walk-a-thon was almost a success, too. But the day before, Principal Dorsey called me into his office. He wanted to know if it was true that I had been telling people that the money would go to cancer research, because he had understood the money was going to our 8th grade graduation party. I didn't answer. He said that he was going to call some of the people who pledged money to ask them if I had said anything about cancer.

"It was the only way I could raise enough money!" I answered back, knowing the lie had caught up with me.

"Well, it was the wrong thing to do." Principal Dorsey replied. "Now, you are going to have to contact every person who donated and let them know the truth. You also may not have enough money for a graduation party now."

I knew I should never have volunteered to lead this.

10.   Which is the best summary of the story?

    Ⓐ   Student Council members learn that they do not have enough money for an 8th grade graduation ceremony. They decide to raise money through a walk-a-thon which the narrator volunteers to lead.

    Ⓑ   Student Council members learn that they do not have enough money for an 8th grade graduation ceremony. They decide to raise money through a walk-a-thon which the narrator volunteers to lead. Fund raising doesn't go as well as anticipated and the 8th grade graduation party is in jeopardy. The Student Council members were probably really mad after all their hard work.

    Ⓒ   The 8th grade class did not have enough money for a graduation party. They tried to raise money, but failed.

    Ⓓ   Student Council members learn that they do not have enough money for an 8th grade graduation ceremony. They decide to raise money through a walk-a-thon which the narrator volunteers to lead. Fund raising doesn't go as well as anticipated and the 8th grade graduation party is in jeopardy.

© Lumos Information Services 2016 | LumosLearning.com

Lesson 5: Plot (RL.8.2)

1. **What are the elements of plot?**

    (A) prelude, beginning, interlude, middle, end

    (B) introduction, setting, action, conflict, falling action

    (C) introduction, rising action, climax, falling action, resolution

    (D) beginning, middle, end

2. **What are the two main types of conflict?**

    (A) internal and external

    (B) interior and exterior

    (C) good and bad

    (D) big and little

3. **What is the plot of a story?**

    (A) the message that the author is trying to convey

    (B) the series of events that make up the story

    (C) the use of characters in a story

    (D) the part of a story where the characters decide what they are going to do

Walk-A-Thon

It was clear there weren't enough funds for the 8th-grade graduation ceremony at the end of the year. Big deal – why should I care? I was on the student council, but I never cared about graduation ceremonies.

It costs about $5,000.00 for the rent, equipment, the insurance and all the other incidentals that pile up when planning a large event. Principal Dorsey told us that he didn't have the money this year. He said that if we wanted to keep the graduation tradition going, we would have to raise the money ourselves. "I'm sure we can live without the ceremony, but it would be nice to have," he told us. Then he left the meeting.

Immediately, Katrina Reynolds shot her hand in the air. She's not very popular, and I always feel kind of sorry for her. "We have to do this, you guys," Katrina gushed. "There is no way we are going to be the only class ever not to have a graduation ceremony."

Then, of course, Abbie Morelle, who was President, shot her hand in the air. I'd been on Student Council for two years, and as far as I could remember, Abbie had never let Katrina say anything without disagreeing with it. "It's very late in the year," Abbie said. "And we already have the Band Land Dance scheduled, which we don't have enough money for. We can't raise $7,000 in, like, two months."

Paulie Roman, who was treasurer, said, "According to my records it would be more like $7,012, although we can't be certain of the precise cost of unspecified expenses related to the ceremony."

I didn't care. To me, 8th grade is pure misery, no matter what you do. If you have a great graduation ceremony at the end of it, that's like saying, "We had such a great time in all of our boring classes and with all of the bullies every day. Let's have a party to celebrate them!" But I was all for a fundraiser if it would get Abbie Morelle off Katrina's back.

I said, "Let's do a walk-a-thon. We could raise a lot of money that way."

"Walk-a-thons are stupid," Abbie said.

Paulie Roman asked, "How much money could we raise with a walk-a-thon?"

I said, "When we did a walk-a-thon for cancer research in elementary school, we raised $4,000. This school is twice as big, and people can walk farther."

"Yeah," Abbie said, "but that was for cancer. Why would anyone give us money for a graduation ceremony? Plus, someone has to organize it, and it's complicated."

That got me mad enough that I had to say, "It's not that complicated. I'll do it."

What was I thinking? I spent the next month doing almost nothing except organizing that walk-a-thon. I hate walk-a-thons, and I hate talking to people about money. I ended up doing way more than I ever wanted to.

Within the first two weeks, I could see that we weren't going to get enough. It was because we weren't raising money for something important, like cancer. So I started telling people that the money would also go for cancer research. Then, when I saw how many people were ready to give more, I just told them it was all for cancer research. I got hundreds of parents signed up, and I got businesses to donate food and decorations.

Abbie was completely jealous.

The walk-a-thon was almost a success, too. But the day before, Principal Dorsey called me into his office. He wanted to know if it was true that I had been telling people that the money would go to cancer research because he had understood the money was going or our 8th-grade graduation party. I didn't answer. He said that he was going to call some of the people who pledged money to ask them if I had said anything about cancer.

"It was the only way I could raise enough money!" I answered back, knowing the lie had caught up with me.

"Well, it was the wrong thing to do." Principal Dorsey replied. "Now, you are going to have to contact every person who donated and let them know the truth. You also may not have enough money for a graduation party now."

I knew I should never have volunteered to lead this.

4. **What is the major type of conflict is in this story?**

   Ⓐ   external: man vs fate
   Ⓑ   external: man vs man
   Ⓒ   internal: man vs himself
   Ⓓ   external: man vs nature

5. **What is the conflict in this story?**

   Ⓐ   there is not enough money for an 8th grade graduation party
   Ⓑ   who is most popular
   Ⓒ   who will organize the walk-a-thon
   Ⓓ   whether or not to have graduation

6. **What is the exposition in this story?**

   Ⓐ   I didn't care. To me, 8th grade is pure misery, no matter what you do. If you have a great graduation ceremony at the end of it, that's like saying, "We had such a great time in all of our boring classes, and with all of the bullies every day. Let's have a party to celebrate them!" But I was all for a fundraiser if it would get Abbie Morelle off Katrina's back.
   Ⓑ   He wanted to know if it was true that I had been telling people that the money would go to cancer research, because he had understood the money was going or our 8th grade graduation party.
   Ⓒ   Principal Dorsey told us that he didn't have the money this year. He said that if we wanted to keep the graduation tradition going, we would have to raise the money ourselves.
   Ⓓ   It was clear there weren't enough funds for the 8th grade graduation ceremony at the end of the year. Big deal – why should I care? I was on the Student Council, but I never cared about graduation ceremonies.

7. **What is the most important event in the rising action of this story?**

   Ⓐ   when the narrator volunteers to take charge of the walk-a-thon
   Ⓑ   when the narrator lies about why she is collecting the money
   Ⓒ   when the narrator gets called into the principal's office
   Ⓓ   when the principal says there will be no graduation

8. **What is the climax of this story?**

   Ⓐ   when the narrator volunteers to be in charge of the walk-a-thon
   Ⓑ   when the narrator lies about why she is collecting the money
   Ⓒ   when the principal calls the narrator to the office and the narrator confesses to lying about the cause
   Ⓓ   when the narrator makes Abbie jealous

9. **What is the most important event in the falling action of this story?**

   Ⓐ   when the narrator learns she must contact all the donors
   Ⓑ   when the narrator learns there will be no graduation party
   Ⓒ   when the narrator makes Abbie jealous
   Ⓓ   when the narrator organizes the walk-a-thon

10. **What is the resolution of this story?**

   Ⓐ   when the narrator volunteers to be in charge of the walk-a-thon
   Ⓑ   when the narrator is called to the principal's office
   Ⓒ   when the narrator learns there will be no graduation party
   Ⓓ   when Abbie gets jealous

© Lumos Information Services 2016 | LumosLearning.com

Lesson 6: Setting (RL . 8.2)

1. During which part of a story is the setting usually introduced?

- Ⓐ introduction
- Ⓑ rising action
- Ⓒ climax
- Ⓓ resolution

2. Can there be more than one setting in a story?

- Ⓐ yes
- Ⓑ no
- Ⓒ only if the story is really long
- Ⓓ only if the story is really short

3. Which of the following can convey setting?

- Ⓐ the name of the characters
- Ⓑ the age of the characters
- Ⓒ the culture of the characters
- Ⓓ the thoughts of a character

4. What does the setting tell us about a story?

- Ⓐ the names of the characters
- Ⓑ the time and place of action in the story
- Ⓒ the mood of the story
- Ⓓ one of the above

Megan couldn't believe her luck. She had been standing in line with her best friend Jessica for thirty minutes. Their excitement was mounting as they neared the front of the line for the famed Greased Lightning rollercoaster. Just as they took their seats, the clouds opened up. Soaking wet and disappointed, the girls followed the directions of the ride employees and took shelter under the nearby canopies.

5.   Which of the following does not help the reader to gain a sense of the setting?

Ⓐ   the time of day
Ⓑ   the weather
Ⓒ   the time of year
Ⓓ   the mood of the main character

It had been a year since Lauren had seen Bailey. Bailey's family had moved to Qatar leaving Lauren to face the world without her best friend. Anxiously, Lauren waited at the arrival gate hoping to glimpse a peek at her childhood friend. She knew after eleven hours in the air, Bailey would be exhausted; but, she could hardly wait to catch up. Moments later, the doors to the gate flung open, and there was her best friend, Bailey.

Once home, the hours passed like minutes as the girls laughed and giggled sharing moments from the last year. It felt as if they had never been apart. But Lauren felt like Bailey was holding something back.

6.   What is the primary setting for this passage?

Ⓐ   an airport
Ⓑ   Lauren's house
Ⓒ   Bailey's house
Ⓓ   There is not enough information to determine the setting.

From Chapter 5 of **Peter Pan** by J.M. Barrie

"He lay at his ease in a rough chariot drawn and propelled by his men, and instead of a right hand he had the iron hook with which ever and anon he encouraged them to increase their pace. As dogs this terrible man treated and addressed them, and as dogs they obeyed him. In person he was cadaverous [dead looking] and [dark faced], and his hair was dressed in long curls, which at a little distance looked like black candles, and gave a singularly threatening expression to his handsome countenance. His eyes were of the blue of the forget-me-not, and of a profound melancholy, save when he was plunging his hook into you, at which time two red spots appeared in them and lit them up horribly. A man of indomitable courage, it was said that the only thing he shied at was the sight of his own blood, which was thick and of an unusual color. But undoubtedly the grimmest part of him was his iron claw."

7.   What is the setting of the excerpt?

Ⓐ   a sports arena
Ⓑ   a party on the back of a cruise ship
Ⓒ   a private gathering
Ⓓ   There is not enough information to determine the setting.

The Laundry

Charlie's parents always assigned him chores around the house. They would often ask him to trim the lawn, wash the dishes, and feed the dog. However, his chores never included laundry. He relied on his mother to wash his clothes for him. Charlie was an outstanding student and was recently accepted to a top college. The college he planned to attend was in New York City. Charlie was nervous about leaving Texas, where he grew up, and being so far away from his family; but, he knew that the college in New York was the perfect fit for him. Before he left, his mother decided that she had better show him how to wash his own clothes because she wouldn't be there to do it for him anymore. She showed Charlie how to sort his clothes into two piles: whites and colors.

Then she showed him how much soap to use and told him when to use hot or warm water and when to use cold water. Next, she explained the different settings on the dryer and told him to be careful not to dry certain items on high heat. Charlie didn't pay much attention. He didn't see what could happen or what was so complicated about washing clothes. He planned on packing mostly t-shirts and jeans and figured that it would be hard to mess up something so simple.

When Charlie arrived at school, he was completely overwhelmed with all of the exciting things to do and new people to meet. He was also careful to dedicate plenty of time to his school work because he wanted to impress his professors and earn good grades. One morning Charlie woke up and found that he had no clean clothes to wear. His schedule had been so packed with activities and studying that he

had managed to get through the first month of school without doing any laundry. That night, Charlie piled his soiled clothes into a large basket and headed to his dormitory's laundry room. He shoved all of his clothes into a washer, poured in the soap, and pressed the start. Half an hour later, he opened the washer and started moving the clothes into the dryer. It was then that he realized that he had skipped one very significant step. All of his white t-shirts and socks had turned pink. He had forgotten to sort his colors from his whites. Charlie had received a bright red t-shirt with his new school's logo across the front. The red dye had bled in the wash, turning all of his white clothes pink. Charlie was unhappy about his destroyed wardrobe, but he figured that there was absolutely nothing to do except to put the clothes in the dryer and hope for the best. So he transferred the clothes to a dryer and set the heat to high. After all, he was anxious to get back upstairs to his studies. An hour later, Charlie removed his clothes from the dryer and headed straight back to his dorm room. The following morning, he reached for one of his favorite t-shirts. It was slightly pink now, but he didn't have enough money to replace all of his newly pink clothes. He would have to wear them, pink or not. As he pulled the shirt over his head, he noticed that it seemed tight. He looked at himself in the mirror.

The shirt had shrunk in the dryer. It looked like he had tried to squeeze into his little sister's pink t-shirt. All Charlie could do was laugh. He called his mom and asked her to repeat her laundry instructions again.

This time, Charlie took notes.

8.   What is the first setting of this excerpt?

Ⓐ   Texas
Ⓑ   New York
Ⓒ   a laundromat
(Ⓓ)   There is not enough information to determine the setting.

I sat with my mother, a friendly and courageous woman, on the back porch of our country home. The thermometer read 100 degrees, and even the plants seemed to sweat in the heat.

9.   Which of the following does not help the reader to better understand the setting of the story?

Ⓐ   "the back porch"
Ⓑ   "thermometer read 100 degrees"
Ⓒ   "a friendly and courageous woman"
Ⓓ   "our country home"

University of California Berkeley scientists confirmed that a cluster of fossilized bones found in Silicon Valley are likely the remains of a mammoth. The giant beast would have roamed the area between 10,000 and 40,000 years ago. A pair of elephant-like tusks, a huge pelvic bone, and the animal's rib cage were found by an amateur naturalist who was walking a dog along a canal near San Jose's Guadalupe River. It could be the remains of a Columbian mammoth, according to paleontologists who expect to study the site.

10.   What is the setting of this article?

Ⓐ   Columbia
Ⓑ   University of California Berkeley
Ⓒ   a canal near the Guadalupe River in the Silicon Valley
Ⓓ   Berkeley

Lesson 7: Character (RL.8.2)

1. **What is a round character?**

    (A) a character who has many personality traits
    (B) a character who has very few personality traits
    (C) a character who changes throughout the story
    (D) a character who does not change throughout the story

2. **Who or what is the protagonist of a story?**

    (A) the main character with the problem
    (B) the character that is the least interesting
    (C) the character that is the most interesting
    (D) main character's opposing force

3. **Who or what is the antagonist in a story?**

    (A) the main character of a story
    (B) the main character's opposing force
    (C) the character that is the least interesting
    (D) the character that is the most interesting

4. **What is a static character?**

    (A) a character that changes during the course of the story
    (B) a character that does not change during the course of the story
    (C) a character with a smaller role that is not important to the development of the story
    (D) a character with a large role that is not vital to the development of the story

5. **What is a dynamic character?**

    (A) a character that changes during the course of the story
    (B) a character that does not change during the course of the story
    (C) a character with a smaller role that is not important to the development of the story
    (D) a character with a large role that is not vital to the development of the story

© Lumos Information Services 2016 | LumosLearning.com

Walk-A-Thon

It was clear there weren't enough funds for the 8th-grade graduation ceremony at the end of the year. Big deal – why should I care? I was on the student council, but I never cared about graduation ceremonies.

It costs about $5,000.00 for the rent, equipment, the insurance and all the other incidentals that pile up when planning a large event. Principal Dorsey told us that he didn't have the money this year. He said that if we wanted to keep the graduation tradition going, we would have to raise the money ourselves. "I'm sure we can live without the ceremony, but it would be nice to have," he told us. Then he left the meeting.

Immediately, Katrina Reynolds shot her hand in the air. She's not very popular, and I always feel kind of sorry for her. "We have to do this, you guys," Katrina gushed. "There is no way we are going to be the only class ever not to have a graduation ceremony."

Then, of course, Abbie Morelle, who was President, shot her hand in the air. I'd been on Student Council for two years, and as far as I could remember, Abbie had never let Katrina say anything without disagreeing with it. "It's very late in the year," Abbie said. "And we already have the Band Land Dance scheduled, which we don't have enough money for. We can't raise $7,000 in, like, two months."

Paulie Roman, who was treasurer, said, "According to my records it would be more like $7,012, although we can't be certain of the precise cost of unspecified expenses related to the ceremony."

I didn't care. To me, 8th grade is pure misery, no matter what you do. If you have a great graduation ceremony at the end of it, that's like saying, "We had such a great time in all of our boring classes and with all of the bullies every day. Let's have a party to celebrate them!" But I was all for a fundraiser if it would get Abbie Morelle off Katrina's back.

I said, "Let's do a walk-a-thon. We could raise a lot of money that way."

"Walk-a-thons are stupid," Abbie said.

Paulie Roman asked, "How much money could we raise with a walk-a-thon?"

I said, "When we did a walk-a-thon for cancer research in elementary school, we raised $4,000. This school is twice as big, and people can walk farther."

"Yeah," Abbie said, "but that was for cancer. Why would anyone give us money for a graduation ceremony? Plus, someone has to organize it, and it's complicated."

That got me mad enough that I had to say, "It's not that complicated. I'll do it."

What was I thinking? I spent the next month doing almost nothing except organizing that walk-a-thon.

I hate walk-a-thons, and I hate talking to people about money. I ended up doing way more than I ever wanted to.

Within the first two weeks, I could see that we weren't going to get enough. It was because we weren't raising money for something important, like cancer. So I started telling people that the money would also go for cancer research. Then, when I saw how many people were ready to give more, I just told them it was all for cancer research. I got hundreds of parents signed up, and I got businesses to donate food and decorations.

Abbie was completely jealous.

The walk-a-thon was almost a success, too. But the day before, Principal Dorsey called me into his office. He wanted to know if it was true that I had been telling people that the money would go to cancer research because he had understood the money was going or our 8th-grade graduation party. I didn't answer. He said that he was going to call some of the people who pledged money to ask them if I had said anything about cancer.

"It was the only way I could raise enough money!" I answered back, knowing the lie had caught up with me.

"Well, it was the wrong thing to do." Principal Dorsey replied. "Now, you are going to have to contact every person who donated and let them know the truth. You also may not have enough money for a graduation party now."

I knew I should never have volunteered to lead this.

6.   What sort of character is the narrator?

   Ⓐ   major
   Ⓑ   minor
   Ⓒ   middle
   Ⓓ   weak

© Lumos Information Services 2016 | LumosLearning.com

Excerpt from Stave *One of A Christmas Carol* by Charles Dickens

(1) "What else can I be," returned the uncle [Scrooge], "when I live in such a world of fools as this? Merry Christmas! Out upon Merry Christmas! What's Christmas time to you but a time for paying bills without money; a time for finding yourself a year older, but not an hour richer; a time for balancing your books and having every item in 'em through a round dozen of months presented dead against you? If I could work my will," said Scrooge indignantly, "every idiot who goes about with 'Merry Christmas' on his lips, should be boiled with his own pudding, and buried with a stake of holly through his heart. He should!"

Excerpt from Stave Five of *A Christmas Carol* by Charles Dickens

(2) "A merry Christmas, Bob!" said Scrooge [the uncle], with an earnestness that could not be mistaken, as he clapped him on the back. "A merrier Christmas, Bob, my good fellow, than I have given you, for many a year! I'll raise your salary, and endeavor to assist your struggling family, and we will discuss your affairs this very afternoon, over a Christmas bowl of smoking bishop, Bob! Make up the fires, and buy another coal-scuttle before you dot another, Bob Cratchit!"

7.   What type of characterization does Dickens use to describe Scrooge (the uncle)?

   Ⓐ   indirect characterization
   Ⓑ   direct characterization
   Ⓒ   false characterization
   Ⓓ   none of the above

8.   What type of character is Scrooge (the uncle)?

   Ⓐ   flat
   Ⓑ   static
   Ⓒ   round
   Ⓓ   dynamic

Excerpt from the Foreword of *A Princess of Mars* by Edgar Rice Burroughs

My first recollection of Captain Carter is of the few months he spent at my father's home in Virginia, just prior to the opening of the Civil War. I was then a child of but five years, yet I well remember the tall, dark, smooth-faced, athletic man whom I called Uncle Jack.

He seemed always to be laughing; and he entered into the sports of the children with the same hearty good fellowship he displayed toward those pastimes in which the men and women of his own age indulged; or he would sit for an hour at a time entertaining my old grandmother with stories of his strange, wild life in all parts of the world. We all loved him, and our slaves fairly worshipped the ground he trod.

He was a splendid specimen of manhood, standing a good two inches over six feet, broad of shoulder and narrow of hip, with the carriage of the trained fighting man. His features were regular and clear cut, his hair black and closely cropped, while his eyes were of a steel gray, reflecting a strong and loyal character, filled with fire and initiative. His manners were perfect, and his courtliness was that of a typical southern gentleman of the highest type.

His horsemanship, especially after hounds, was a marvel and delight even in that country of magnificent horsemen. I have often heard my father caution him against his wild recklessness, but he would only laugh, and say that the tumble that killed him would be from the back of a horse yet unfoaled.

When the war broke out he left us, nor did I see him again for some fifteen or sixteen years. When he returned it was without warning, and I was much surprised to note that he had not aged apparently a moment, nor had he changed in any other outward way. He was, when others were with him, the same genial, happy fellow we had known of old, but when he thought himself alone I have seen him sit for hours gazing off into space, his face set in a look of wistful longing and hopeless misery; and at night he would sit thus looking up into the heavens, at what I did not know until I read his manuscript years afterward.

9.   **What sort of characterization is used in this excerpt?**

   (A) direct characterization
   (B) indirect characterization
   (C) false characterization
   (D) none of the above

10. **What type of character is Captain Carter?**

   (A) flat
   (B) static
   (C) round
   (D) dynamic

© Lumos Information Services 2016 | LumosLearning.com

Lesson 8: Analyzing Literature (RL.8.3)

The Laundry

Charlie's parents always assigned him chores around the house. They would often ask him to trim the lawn, wash the dishes, and feed the dog. However, his chores never included laundry. He relied on his mother to wash his clothes for him. Charlie was an outstanding student and was recently accepted to a top college. The college he planned to attend was in New York City. Charlie was nervous about leaving Texas, where he grew up, and being so far away from his family; but, he knew that the college in New York was the perfect fit for him. Before he left, his mother decided that she had better show him how to wash his own clothes because she wouldn't be there to do it for him anymore. She showed Charlie how to sort his clothes into two piles: whites and colors.

Then she showed him how much soap to use and told him when to use hot or warm water and when to use cold water. Next, she explained the different settings on the dryer and told him to be careful not to dry certain items on high heat. Charlie didn't pay much attention. He didn't see what could happen or what was so complicated about washing clothes. He planned on packing mostly t-shirts and jeans and figured that it would be hard to mess up something so simple.

When Charlie arrived at school, he was completely overwhelmed with all of the exciting things to do and new people to meet. He was also careful to dedicate plenty of time to his school work because he wanted to impress his professors and earn good grades. One morning Charlie woke up and found that he had no clean clothes to wear. His schedule had been so packed with activities and studying that he had managed to get through the first month of school without doing any laundry. That night, Charlie piled his soiled clothes into a large basket and headed to his dormitory's laundry room. He shoved all of his clothes into a washer, poured in the soap, and pressed the start. Half an hour later, he opened the washer and started moving the clothes into the dryer. It was then that he realized that he had skipped one very significant step. All of his white t-shirts and socks had turned pink. He had forgotten to sort his colors from his whites. Charlie had received a bright red t-shirt with his new school's logo across the front. The red dye had bled in the wash, turning all of his white clothes pink. Charlie was unhappy about his destroyed wardrobe, but he figured that there was absolutely nothing to do except to put the clothes in the dryer and hope for the best. So he transferred the clothes to a dryer and set the heat to high. After all, he was anxious to get back upstairs to his studies. An hour later, Charlie removed his clothes from the dryer and headed straight back to his dorm room. The following morning, he reached for one of his favorite t-shirts. It was slightly pink now, but he didn't have enough money to replace all of his newly pink clothes. He would have to wear them, pink or not. As he pulled the shirt over his head, he noticed that it seemed tight. He looked at himself in the mirror.

The shirt had shrunk in the dryer. It looked like he had tried to squeeze into his little sister's pink t-shirt. All Charlie could do was laugh. He called his mom and asked her to repeat her laundry instructions again.

This time, Charlie took notes.

1. **Which statement best describes Charlie's parents' expectations of him?**

    Ⓐ They let Charlie do whatever he wants since he's smart and will probably make good decisions.

    Ⓑ They expect Charlie to help around the house and earn good grades in school.

    Ⓒ They don't expect much from Charlie since he probably won't fulfill their expectations.

    Ⓓ They expect Charlie to do all the work around the house while earning straight A's.

2. **After Charlie had a mishap with his laundry, he laughed. What does this reveal about Charlie's character?**

    Ⓐ Charlie is the kind of person who realizes what's done is done; all he can do is try again.

    Ⓑ Charlie is the kind of person who laughs wildly when he isn't sure how to react to stressful situations.

    Ⓒ Charlie is the kind of person who laughs at the misfortune of others.

    Ⓓ Charlie is the kind of person who laughs when he isn't sure what to do.

Excerpt from Stave Five of *A Christmas Carol* by Charles Dickens

(2) "A merry Christmas, Bob!" said Scrooge [the uncle], with an earnestness that could not be mistaken, as he clapped him on the back. "A merrier Christmas, Bob, my good fellow, than I have given you, for many a year! I'll raise your salary, and endeavor to assist your struggling family, and we will discuss your affairs this very afternoon, over a Christmas bowl of smoking bishop, Bob! Make up the fires, and buy another coal-scuttle before you dot another, Bob Cratchit!"

3. **What is the significance of this dialogue?**

    Ⓐ This dialogue is significant because it shows that Scrooge wants to wish the person he's addressing a Merry Christmas.

    Ⓑ This dialogue is significant because it is important for the reader to know Scrooge's feelings about Christmas.

    Ⓒ This dialogue is significant because Scrooge wants to make sure everyone knows he dislikes Christmas.

    Ⓓ This dialogue is significant because it shows Scrooge cannot wait for Christmas morning to come, so he can rip open his presents.

© Lumos Information Services 2016 | LumosLearning.com

4.   What is the significance of this dialogue?

   Ⓐ It allows the reader to really understand the change that Scrooge underwent in the story.
   Ⓑ It allows the reader to see that Scrooge liked Christmas all along.
   Ⓒ It allows the reader to see that nothing could change Scrooge's opinion of Christmas.
   Ⓓ none of the above

5.   Why is it important to understand what characters can reveal to readers?

   Ⓐ It allows readers to see and understand how characters interact with the setting.
   Ⓑ It allows readers to see and understand how characters interact with other characters.
   Ⓒ It allows readers to see and understand how the actions of a character can drive the plot.
   Ⓓ all of the above

Casey Jones

A Tennessee Legend

retold by S.E. Schlosser

Casey Jones, that heroic railroad engineer of the Cannonball, was known as the man who always brought the train in on time. He would blow the whistle so it started off soft but would increase to a wail louder than a banshee before dying off. Got so as people would recognize that whistle and know when Casey was driving past.

April 29, 1900, Casey brought the Cannonball into Memphis dead on time. As he was leaving, he found out one of the other engineers was sick and unable to make his run. So Casey volunteered to help out his friend. He pulled the train out of the station about eleven p.m., an hour and thirty-five minutes late. Casey was determined to make up the time. As soon as he could, he highballed out of Memphis (highballing means to go very fast and take a lot of risks to get where your headed) and started making up for lost time.

About four a.m., when he had nearly made up all the time on the run, Casey rounded a corner near Vaughin, Mississippi and saw a stalled freight train on the track. He shouted for his fireman to jump. The fireman made it out alive, but Casey Jones died in the wreck, one hand on the brake and one on the whistle chord.

6.   Which of the statements below best describes Casey Jones?

Ⓐ   He was a large, friendly man known to most as the Cannonball.

Ⓑ   He was a courageous, and punctual man.

Ⓒ   He was so concerned about being punctual, he was not careful when driving.

Ⓓ   none of the above

7.   What do Casey's actions in the last paragraph reveal about him?

Ⓐ   He wasn't very smart because he didn't jump off the train in time.

Ⓑ   Up to his very last act, he was courageous and thinking of others before himself.

Ⓒ   Up to his very last act, he was courageous.

Ⓓ   none of the above

The Grasshopper and the Ants

Aesop's Fable

In a field, one summer's day, a grasshopper was hopping about, chirping and singing to its heart's content. A group of ants walked by, grunting as they struggled to carry plump kernels of corn. "Where are you going with those heavy things?" asked the grasshopper. Without stopping, the first ant replied, "To our ant hill. This is the third kernel I've delivered today."

"Why not come and sing with me," teased the grasshopper, "instead of working so hard?"

"We are helping to store food for the winter," said the ant, "and think you should do the same."

"Winter is far away and it is a glorious day to play," sang the grasshopper. But the ants went on their way and continued their hard work.

The weather soon turned cold. All the food lying in the field was covered with a thick white blanket of snow that even the grasshopper could not dig through.

© Lumos Information Services 2016 | LumosLearning.com

Soon the grasshopper found itself dying of hunger. He staggered to the ants' hill and saw them handing out corn from the stores they had collected in the summer. He begged them for something to eat.

"What!" cried the ants in surprise, "haven't you stored anything away for the winter? What in the world were you doing all last summer?"

"I didn't have time to store any food," complained the grasshopper; "I was so busy playing music that before I knew it the summer was gone."

The ants shook their heads in disgust, turned their backs on the grasshopper and went on with their work.

8.   **What does the response of the first ant to the grasshopper reveal for readers?**

     Ⓐ He is taking his work seriously.
     Ⓑ He doesn't like grasshoppers.
     Ⓒ He likes to work alone.
     Ⓓ He has just started working and doesn't want to be bothered.

9.   **What does the grasshopper's response to the ant reveal about the grasshopper?**

     Ⓐ He is trying to be responsible.
     Ⓑ He is afraid of the ant.
     Ⓒ He is not very responsible.
     Ⓓ He is very similar to the ant.

10. **What do the ants' response to the grasshopper reveal about the ants' opinion of the grasshopper's work?**

     Ⓐ They are proud of what the grasshopper has done.
     Ⓑ They want to become friendlier with the grasshopper.
     Ⓒ They are unsure of what to say to the grasshopper.
     Ⓓ They can't believe the grasshopper would be so careless.

Craft and Structure

Lesson 9: Meaning and Tone (RL .8.4)

1. **What is the tone of a piece of literature?**

    Ⓐ the rhythm of the words when read out loud
    Ⓑ the level of sound with which it should be read
    Ⓒ the author's attitude about the subject and/or the readers
    Ⓓ none of the above

Tonight's homework is to read thirty pages in the textbook.

2. **What is the tone of this sentence?**

    Ⓐ neutral
    Ⓑ dramatic
    Ⓒ angry
    Ⓓ friendly

Oh great! My thoughtful teacher gave us homework again tonight! Sure, I have nothing better to do than read thirty pages out of an outdated textbook. I don't have a life.

3. **What is the tone?**

    Ⓐ expectant
    Ⓑ sad
    Ⓒ sarcastic
    Ⓓ adoring

I simply cannot believe that after all the reading we have done this week, we have to read thirty pages tonight. This is an outrage!

4.   What is the tone?

   (A) angry
   (B) gleeful
   (C) skeptical
   (D) questioning

Excerpt from *Because of Winn-Dixie*

by Kate DiCamillo

The Open Arms had mice. They were there from when it was a Pick-It-Quick and there were lots of good things to eat in the building, and when the Pick-It-Quick became the Open Arms Baptist Church of Naomi, the mice stayed around to eat all the leftover crumbs from the potluck suppers. The preacher kept on saying he was going to have to do something about them, but he never did. Because the truth is, he couldn't stand the thought of hurting anything, even a mouse.

Well, Winn-Dixie saw that mouse, and he was up and after him. One minute, everything was quiet and serious and the preacher was going on and on and on; and the next minute, Winn-Dixie looked like a furry bullet, shooting across the building, chasing that mouse. He was barking and his feet were skidding all over the polished Pick-It-Quick floor, and people were clapping and hollering and pointing. They really went wild when Winn-Dixie actually caught the mouse.

5.   What is the tone in this excerpt?

   (A) romantic
   (B) unemotional
   (C) enthusiastic
   (D) morose

From **Narrative of the Life of Frederick Douglass, an American Slave**

This battle with Mr. Covey was the turning point in my career as a slave. It rekindled the few expiring embers of freedom, and revived within me a sense of my own manhood.

6.   **What is the tone of the statement above?**

(A) encouraging
(B) sarcastic
(C) unemotional
(D) sorrowful

Excerpt from "**The Story of the Wild Huntsman**" by Heinrich Hoffmann

This is the Wild Huntsman that shoots the hares

With the grass-green coat he always wears:

With game-bag, powder-horn and gun,

He's going out to have some fun.

He finds it hard, without a pair

Of spectacles, to shoot the hare:

He put his spectacles upon his nose, and said,

"Now I will shoot the hares, and kill them dead."

The hare sits snug in leaves and grass

And laughs to see the green man pass

7.   **What is the tone of this excerpt?**

(A) joyous
(B) formal
(C) serious
(D) comical

8.   **In this sentence, what does "snug" most likely mean?**

   Ⓐ   seaworthiness
   Ⓑ   fitting closely
   Ⓒ   privacy
   Ⓓ   humorous

9.   **In this excerpt, what does "spectacles" most likely means?**

   Ⓐ   something unusual
   Ⓑ   something one would be curious about
   Ⓒ   dramatic display
   Ⓓ   glasses

The Ungrateful Son

By Jacob and Wilhelm Grimm

Once a man was sitting with his wife before their front door. They had a roasted chicken which they were about to eat together. Then the man saw that his aged father was approaching, and he hastily took the chicken and hid it, for he did not want to share it with him. The old man came, had a drink, and went away. Now the son wanted to put the roasted chicken back onto the table, but when he reached for it, it had turned into a large toad, which jumped into his face and sat there and never went away again. If anyone tried to remove it, it looked venomously at him as though it would jump into his face, so that no one dared to touch it. And the ungrateful son was forced to feed the toad every day, or else it would eat from his face. And thus he went to and fro in the world without rest.

10. **In this story, what does "hastily" most likely means?**

   Ⓐ   hurriedly
   Ⓑ   slowly
   Ⓒ   carefully
   Ⓓ   quietly

Lesson 10: Compare and Contrast (RL . 8.5)

1.   **When you are comparing two things, what are you looking for?**

     Ⓐ   similarities
     Ⓑ   differences
     Ⓒ   similarities and differences
     Ⓓ   none of the above

2.   **Which of the following group of signal words would you most likely find in a paper comparing two things?**

     Ⓐ   in addition, finally, above all
     Ⓑ   meanwhile, coupled with, for instance
     Ⓒ   likewise, as well, the same as
     Ⓓ   although, however, contrary to

3.   **Which of the following graphic organizers is most effectively used to compare and contrast?**

     Ⓐ   Venn diagram
     Ⓑ   brace map
     Ⓒ   fish bone map
     Ⓓ   tree map

4.   **When you are contrasting two things, what are you looking for?**

     Ⓐ   similarities
     Ⓑ   differences
     Ⓒ   similarities and differences
     Ⓓ   none of the above

5.   **In a Venn diagram, where does the "common" information belong?**

     Ⓐ   in the middle
     Ⓑ   on the right
     Ⓒ   on the left
     Ⓓ   no where

© Lumos Information Services 2016 | LumosLearning.com

6.   **Which of the following group of signal words would you most likely find in a paper contrasting two things?**

    Ⓐ   in addition, finally, above all

    Ⓑ   meanwhile, coupled with, for instance

    Ⓒ   likewise, as well, the same as

    Ⓓ   although, however, contrary to

"The Eagle"	"The First Flight"
Far from the habitations of humans and their petty quarrels, there once lived on top of a rugged hill, an old eagle. When the fragrant morning breeze blew through his nest, the eagle would shake his feathers and spread out his wings. When the sun rose high and the world below engaged itself in its unceasing fight for survival, the eagle would take off from the hilltop and circle majestically over the valley and its dwellers, the fields and the running brooks. If he saw something worthwhile, such as a hare or a rat, a pigeon or a chick, he would swoop down on it like lightning, fetch it to his nest, and devour it. He would then inspect the surroundings once again.	The young seagull was alone on his ledge. His two brothers and his sister had a already flown away the day before. He had been afraid to fly with them. Somehow, when he had taken a little run forward to the brink of the ledge and attempted to flap his wings he became afraid. The great expanse of sea stretched down beneath, and it was such a long way down, miles down. He felt certain that his wings would never support him; so he bent his head and ran away, back to the little hole under the ledge where he slept at night. Even when each of his brothers and his little sister, whose wings were far shorter than his own, ran to the brink, flapped their wings, and flew away, he failed to muster up courage to take that plunge, which appeared to him so desperate. His father and mother had come around calling to him shrilly, upbraiding him, and threatening to let him starve on his ledge unless he flew away; but for the life of him he could not move.

7.   **After reading the two passages, what contrast can be made?**

    Ⓐ   Passage one is about an eagle and passage two is about a seagull.

    Ⓑ   The eagle is old and the seagull is young.

    Ⓒ   The old eagle has mastered flying whereas the young seagull is afraid of flying.

    Ⓓ   all of the above

8. **While the eagle is a confident flyer, what can be noted about the seagull?**

    Ⓐ It is afraid to fly
    Ⓑ It is also a confident flyer
    Ⓒ It is a smaller bird
    Ⓓ It is excited to fly

9. **In what passages is the process of learning to fly discussed?**

    Ⓐ both passages
    Ⓑ neither passage
    Ⓒ "The Eagle"
    Ⓓ "The First Flight"

10. **According to the two passages, what does flying enable both the eagle and the seagull to do?**

    Ⓐ see family
    Ⓑ overcome fears
    Ⓒ eat
    Ⓓ discover new areas

Lesson 11: Producing Suspense and Humor (RL.8.6)

1. **Which of the following is an example of a pun?**

   Ⓐ A boiled egg every morning is hard to beat.
   Ⓑ Nicholas went to buy some camouflage pants the other day, but he couldn't find any.
   Ⓒ Our social studies teacher says her globe means the world to her.
   Ⓓ all of the above

2. **What literary elements can add humor to a story?**

   Ⓐ pun
   Ⓑ setting or situation
   Ⓒ irony
   Ⓓ all of the above

3. **What is the best definition of irony?**

   Ⓐ interesting dialogue between characters
   Ⓑ a scene in which something is complex and difficult to understand
   Ⓒ surprising, funny, or interesting contradictions
   Ⓓ a line that is straight to the point

Excerpt from **The Story of the Wild Huntsman** by Heinrich Hoffmann

This is the Wild Huntsman that shoots the hares

With the grass-green coat he always wears:

With game-bag, powder-horn and gun,

He's going out to have some fun.

He finds it hard, without a pair

Of spectacles, to shoot the hare:

He put his spectacles upon his nose, and said,

"Now I will shoot the hares, and kill them dead."

The hare sits snug in leaves and grass

And laughs to see the green man pass

4. The author creates humor through his description of _____.

    Ⓐ the laughing rabbit

    Ⓑ the hunter who is excited to kill a rabbit

    Ⓒ the hunter who is over-prepared to hunt

    Ⓓ the description of the spectacle

It was a cold and windy evening. The clouds had a haunting presence in the sky. Cindy walked briskly down the street, conscious of the quiet around her. As she approached her front door, she noticed something wasn't right. There was a light on inside, and she thought she could hear someone running down the stairs. Her husband, however, wasn't due home for a couple of hours.

5. This description builds a sense of _____.

    Ⓐ irony

    Ⓑ suspense

    Ⓒ humor

    Ⓓ confusion

In the story *Romeo and Juliet* by William Shakespeare, Romeo commits suicide because he thinks that Juliet is dead. However, the reader knows that she is just in a deep sleep because she took a potion that made her appear dead.

6. What type of irony does Shakespeare use?

    Ⓐ dramatic irony

    Ⓑ verbal irony

    Ⓒ situational irony

    Ⓓ none of the above

A man wakes up early to wash his car before a trip to the park to watch a baseball game. After the game, he realizes that he parked under a tree filled with birds and now his car is covered in white splattered patches. The man said with a loud sigh, "Gee, I sure am glad I woke up early to wash my car."

7.   What type of irony does the author use?

- Ⓐ   dramatic irony
- Ⓑ   verbal irony
- Ⓒ   situational irony
- Ⓓ   none of the above

During a ceremony to release two rehabilitated seals into the ocean, the seals are attacked and killed by whales.

8.   What type of irony does the author use?

- Ⓐ   dramatic irony
- Ⓑ   verbal irony
- Ⓒ   situational irony
- Ⓓ   none of the above

Caitlin saved for years to be able to afford her dream vacation to Tahiti. The morning of her flight she received a phone call from a talk show. If she answered the question correctly she would win a vacation. To her surprise, she answered the question correctly, and the host announced she had won an all-expense paid vacation to Tahiti.

9.   What type of irony does the author use?

- Ⓐ   situational irony
- Ⓑ   verbal irony
- Ⓒ   dramatic irony
- Ⓓ   all of the above

Kyle knew he needed to study for his biology test, but he was so close to beating the next level of his video game that he just couldn't tear himself away from the screen. An hour later, his mom came into his room and said, "Kyle, when you are finished the very important task of beating this level, why don't you consider opening up your binder and studying for your biology test?"

10.   What type of irony does the author use?

- **A**   situational irony
- **B**   verbal irony
- **C**   dramatic irony
- **D**   building suspense

Integration of Knowledge and Ideas

Lesson 12: Media and Literature (RL.8.7)

Casey Jones

A Tennessee Legend

retold by S.E. Schlosser

Casey Jones, that heroic railroad engineer of the Cannonball, was known as the man who always brought the train in on time. He would blow the whistle, so it started off soft but would increase to a wail louder than a banshee before dying off. Got so as people would recognize that whistle and know when Casey was driving past.

April 29, 1900, Casey brought the Cannonball into Memphis dead on time. As he was leaving, he found out one of the other engineers was sick and unable to make his run. So Casey volunteered to help out his friend. He pulled the train out of the station about eleven p.m., an hour and thirty-five minutes late. Casey was determined to make up the time. As soon as he could, he highballed out of Memphis (highballing means to go very fast and take a lot of risks to get where you are headed) and started making up for lost time.

About four a.m., when he had nearly made up all the time on the run, Casey rounded a corner near Vaughn, Mississippi and saw a stalled freight train on the track. He shouted for his fireman to jump. The fireman made it out alive, but Casey Jones died in the wreck, one hand on the brake and one on the whistle chord.

1.   **What medium of publication would be best to use if you wanted to make it possible for people to see Casey Jones operating the train?**

   Ⓐ   a video
   Ⓑ   digital text
   Ⓒ   a traditional book
   Ⓓ   none of the above

2. **What are the advantages of using media to present a particular topic or idea?**

    Ⓐ It can create a picture for viewers to see
    Ⓑ It provides a clear voice for viewers to hear
    Ⓒ both A and B
    Ⓓ none of the above

3. **If you want to see one person's visual interpretation of a character's appearance, what medium of publication would be best to use?**

    Ⓐ movie version of a text
    Ⓑ print text
    Ⓒ digital text
    Ⓓ none of the above

4. **What is multimedia?**

    Ⓐ a medium used to present information
    Ⓑ using more than one medium of expression or communication.
    Ⓒ multiple books
    Ⓓ none of the above

5. **What medium of publication would be best to quickly publish your opinion about a current topic?**

    Ⓐ research paper
    Ⓑ newspaper article
    Ⓒ blog
    Ⓓ none of the above

6. **What is the difference between an article written in a newspaper and a blog post?**

    Ⓐ Newspapers are available only in printed format whereas blogs are published online.
    Ⓑ Newspaper articles are reliable resources while blogs are opinions.
    Ⓒ Blogs have to be proven true, and newspapers do not.
    Ⓓ none of the above

The Lake Isle of Innisfree

I will arise and go now, and go to Innisfree,

And a small cabin build there, of clay and wattles made:

Nine bean-rows will I have there, a hive for the honey-bee;

And live alone in the bee-loud glade.

And I shall have some peace there, for peace comes dropping slow,

Dropping from the veils of the morning to where the cricket sings;

There midnight's all a glimmer, and noon a purple glow,

And evening full of the linnet's wings.

I will arise and go now, for always night and day

I hear lake water lapping with low sounds by the shore;

While I stand on the roadway, or on the pavements grey,

I hear it in the deep heart's core.

W.B. Yeats

About the poet:

William Butler Yeats was an Irish poet and a dramatist. He was one of the foremost figures of 20th century literature and was the driving force behind the Irish literary revival. Together with Lady Gregory and Edward Martin, Yeats founded the Abbey Theater. He served as its chief during its early years and was a pillar of the Irish literary establishment in his later years.

The above well-known poem explores the poet's longing for the peace and tranquility of Innisfree, a place where he spent a lot of time as a boy. This poem is a lyric.

7. **Which medium of publication, the poem or the picture, gives you a better visualization of the lake?**

   Ⓐ the picture
   Ⓑ the poem
   Ⓒ neither
   Ⓓ both

8. **Which medium of publication, the poem or the picture, appeals to more than one of the five senses?**

   Ⓐ the picture
   Ⓑ the poem
   Ⓒ neither
   Ⓓ both

9. **Which medium of publication, the poem or the picture, is the best to visualize the lake and its surroundings?**

   Ⓐ the picture
   Ⓑ the poem
   Ⓒ neither
   Ⓓ both

10. **Which medium of publication, the poem or the picture, would be best to use on a travel brochure to attract people to the lake?**

   Ⓐ the picture
   Ⓑ the poem
   Ⓒ neither
   Ⓓ both

© Lumos Information Services 2016 | LumosLearning.com

Lesson 13: Modern Fictions and Traditional Stories (RL .8.9)

1.   What is a motif?

Ⓐ   the major characters in the story
Ⓑ   how the story ends
Ⓒ   the plot
Ⓓ   a recurring element or idea in a story

2.   Which of the following is a popular motif in traditional stories?

Ⓐ   good vs. evil
Ⓑ   a test of courage
Ⓒ   children who are heroes
Ⓓ   all of the above

The Ant and the Grasshopper

Aesop's Fable

In a field, one summer's day, a grasshopper was hopping about, chirping and singing to its heart's content. A group of ants walked by, grunting as they struggled to carry plump kernels of corn. "Where are you going with those heavy things?" asked the grasshopper.

Without stopping, the first ant replied, "To our ant hill. This is the third kernel I've delivered today."

"Why not come and sing with me," teased the grasshopper, "instead of working so hard?"

"We are helping to store food for the winter," said the ant, "and think you should do the same."

"Winter is far away and it is a glorious day to play," sang the grasshopper. But the ants went on their way and continued their hard work.

The weather soon turned cold. All the food lying in the field was covered with a thick white blanket of snow that even the grasshopper could not dig through.

Soon the grasshopper found itself dying of hunger. He staggered to the ants' hill and saw them handing out corn from the stores they had collected in the summer. He begged them for something to eat.

"What!" cried the ants in surprise, "haven't you stored anything away for the winter? What in the world were you doing all last summer?"

"I didn't have time to store any food," complained the grasshopper; "I was so busy playing music that before I knew it the summer was gone."

The ants shook their heads in disgust, turned their backs on the grasshopper and went on with their work.

3.   What is the lesson of this fable?

Ⓐ   It's okay to have fun.

Ⓑ   Do not help those around you.

Ⓒ   Work hard to prepare for the future.

Ⓓ   Listen to what you are told.

4.   What type of story is "The Ant and the Grasshopper"?

Ⓐ   a fairy tale

Ⓑ   a fable

Ⓒ   a myth

Ⓓ   folktale

5.   How does the reader know "The Ant and the Grasshopper" is a fable?

Ⓐ   Animal characters play the role of humans.

Ⓑ   There is a moral or lesson.

Ⓒ   The story is short.

Ⓓ   all of the above

6.   When someone declares an event to be a "modern day Cinderella story" what do they mean ?

Ⓐ   someone poor or common becomes successful

Ⓑ   someone has evil step-sisters

Ⓒ   someone rides a carriage

Ⓓ   someone is the most beautiful in her family

© Lumos Information Services 2016 | LumosLearning.com

There is a boy who has three brothers. His bike is broken so he goes to borrow one of his brother's. His oldest brother's bike is way too big. His younger brother's bike still has training wheels on it and is too small. His second oldest brother's bike works perfectly though, and that is the one he borrowed.

7.   What traditional story does this remind you of?

Ⓐ   "Little Red Riding Hood"

Ⓑ   The Story of "Goldilocks and the Three Bears"

Ⓒ   "Rumpelstiltskin"

Ⓓ   "Snow White and the Seven Dwarfs"

You read a story about a young girl who battles against all odds to overcome the hardships of homelessness and discrimination to go to Harvard and become extremely successful.

8.   What is a popular motif in this story?

Ⓐ   good vs. evil

Ⓑ   a test of courage

Ⓒ   children who are heroes

Ⓓ   true love

9.   In the classic fairy tale "Cinderella," what do the characters of Cinderella and the stepmother stand for?

Ⓐ   fun vs. boring

Ⓑ   good vs. evil

Ⓒ   young vs. old

Ⓓ   traditional vs. non-traditional

Casey Jones

A Tennessee Legend

retold by S.E. Schlosser

Casey Jones, that heroic railroad engineer of the Cannonball, was known as the man who always brought the train in on time. He would blow the whistle, so it started off soft but would increase to a wail louder than a banshee before dying off. Got so as people would recognize that whistle and know when Casey was driving past.

April 29, 1900, Casey brought the Cannonball into Memphis dead on time. As he was leaving, he found out one of the other engineers was sick and unable to make his run. So Casey volunteered to help out his friend. He pulled the train out of the station about eleven p.m., an hour and thirty-five minutes late. Casey was determined to make up the time. As soon as he could, he highballed out of Memphis (highballing means to go very fast and take a lot of risks to get where you are headed) and started making up for lost time.

About four a.m., when he had nearly made up all the time on the run, Casey rounded a corner near Vaughn, Mississippi and saw a stalled freight train on the track. He shouted for his fireman to jump. The fireman made it out alive, but Casey Jones died in the wreck, one hand on the brake and one on the whistle chord.

10. **What type of story is Casey Jones?**

   Ⓐ fairy tale
   Ⓑ fable
   Ⓒ myth
   Ⓓ folktale

End of Reading: Literature

Reading: Literature

Answer Key
&
Detailed Explanations

Lesson 1: Textual Evidence (RL.8.1)

Question	Answer	Detailed Explanation
1.	B	Answer choice B is correct and can be found in the last sentence of the second paragraph. The other choices are incorrect because they do not indicate change or time.
2.	C	Answer choice C is correct and directly stated in the last two lines of the poem. Answer choice D is incorrect. While the poet does recognize gold is good, he states sympathy is greater. Answer choices A and B do not provide evidence to support the question.
3.	A	Answer choice A is correct because the first line of the poem indicates the poet's sorrow. The other answer choices are incorrect as there is no evidence in the first stanza to support them.
4.	D	Answer choice D is correct because it tells the reader the Montgolfier brothers did indeed build and launch a hot air balloon in 1783. Answer choices A and B are incorrect because they explain how the brothers conceived the idea of a hot air balloon, but they do not state that one was yet created. Answer choice C is incorrect because it simply gives a brief biography of the brothers.
5.	B	Answer choice B is correct because it explains how the Montgolfier brothers used the heat from the fire to propel the bag upwards. Answer choice A describes the materials used to create the first hot air balloon. Answer choice C tells the readers when the first hot air balloon was launched. Answer choice D explains how Joseph Montgolfier generated the idea of using hot air to lift an object.
6.	B	Answer choice B is correct because it shows how Joseph observed something as small as pieces of paper floating up the chimney. Answer choice A is incorrect because it describes the materials used to build the balloon. Answer choice C is incorrect because there is no text evidence to support this answer. The passage does not indicate that the Montgolfier's village was the best place to launch their balloon. Answer choice D is incorrect because it simply gives the reader information about Josepeh Montgolfier's interest in flying.

© Lumos Information Services 2016 | LumosLearning.com

Question	Answer	Detailed Explanation
7.	A	Answer choice A is correct. Text evidence supporting this inference can be found in the line stating the girls were soaking wet and disappointed. They were wet and disappointed because the clouds opened up, meaning it began to rain. There is no evidence to support answer choices B, C or D.
8.	C	Answer choice C is correct. The poet, Yeats, is describing Innisfree as very peaceful and tranquil. All the descriptions that he uses indicate peace and tranquillity. Answer choices A, B and D are incorrect because they are too specific. Each of them is contributes to the overall peace and tranquillity.
9.	A	Answer choice A is correct. The poet is thinking about where he will retire and fondly thinks about Innisfree as he walks to or from work. Answer choices B, C and D cannot be supported by the text.
10.	B	Answer choice B is correct. In the last line of the passage, the narrator tells the reader that Lauren felt like Bailey was holding something back. This means Bailey had a secret she wasn't willing to share. Answer choices A and C are not supported by any evidence in the text.

Lesson 2: Inferences (RL.8.1)

Question	Answer	Detailed Explanation
1.	D	Answer choice D is correct. Patrick was in such a hurry he did not check to see if his bag was in the trunk of his car. His mom realized he had left it and ran out to remind him. There is no evidence to support answer choices A, B, or C.
2.	A	Answer choice A is correct. The word this in the sentence, "he just knew he would make the team this year" indicates that Patrick has tried out before and not made the team. There is no evidence to support answer choices B, C, or D.
3.	B	Answer choice B is correct. Elizabeth was going to drive to work but could not because she did not have her keys. She locked them in the house. Answer choices A and C are not supported in the text.
4.	C	Answer choice C is correct. Samantha's heart pounding loudly, her friendly smile and blushing all indicate she thought the boy was cute. Answer choices A, B and D are not supported by the text. Nothing in the text referred to the boy's backpack, and the boy's actions were not discussed, so the reader cannot draw an inference based on his behavior.
5.	A	Answer choice B is incorrect because Maya realizes the family is needy based on both their actions and the state of their clothes.
6.	C	Answer choice C is correct. Haley is so eager to answer the phone, she doesn't even take a moment to wash the flour off her hands. Answer choice A is incorrect because it is not supported in the text. Answer choice B is incorrect because it is likely Haley doesn't wash her hands because of her eagerness to answer the phone call.
7.	C	Answer choice B is correct because Henry has been saving his money for a year and did research on his destination. Answer choice A is incorrect because Henry has been saving his money, so the trip was planned. Answer choice C is incorrect because Henry did research on his destination. Answer choice D cannot be inferred from the text.

© Lumos Information Services 2016 | LumosLearning.com

Question	Answer	Detailed Explanation
8.	A	Answer choice A is correct. The door was hard to open because it hadn't been opened in quite some time. Additionally, there were cobwebs in the room and dust on the floor meaning no one had entered the room in a long time. Answer choice B is incorrect because it is unlikely a new building would have cobwebs and a layer of dust in it. Answer choice C is incorrect because she was able to get in. The door was not locked, just stuck. Answer choice D is incorrect because there is no evidence to support the inference.
9.	C	Answer choice C is correct. Mark has inherited some the traits and characteristics of his father. Answer choices A, B and D cannot be inferred from the text.
10.	A	Answer choice A is correct. Melody's mom's body language leads the reader to believe she is angry, and her silence and body language indicate she is angry. Answer choice B is incorrect because her body language indicates she is angry, not tired. Answer choice C is incorrect because there is nothing in the passage to lead the reader to believe any dental work was done. Answer choice D is incorrect because there is nothing in the passage to indicate that the kitchen was clean.

Lesson 3: Theme (RL.8.2)

Question	Answer	Detailed Explanation
1.	A	Answer choice A is correct. The theme of a piece is the underlying message of a piece of literature, and the main idea is a statement that tells what the piece is about. Answer choices B, C and D are incorrect and unreasonable.
2.	C	Answer choice C is correct. A universal theme is one that can be found in many stories and pieces of literature and can be applied to any situation, any person or any era. It does not include character names. Answer choices A and D are incorrect. Neither answer is reasonable. Answer choice B is incorrect as the universal theme is not always implicit (not clearly stated). It is sometimes explicit (clearly stated).
3.	D	The first paragraph of the excerpt explains Alice's thoughts that a book is of no use if it doesn't have pictures or conversations. Books with conversations would typically include dialogue which would more often be found in a fiction book.
4.	C	Answer choice C is correct. Readers should look for details in the story to help determine the theme of the story. It also helps to think about what the main character learns. Answer choices A, B, and D are incorrect as they are not ways to help a reader determine the theme of a story.
5.	B	Answer choice B is correct. The reader determines an implied theme of a story through clues in the story. Answer choices A, C, and D are not definitions of an implied theme.
6.	C	Answer choice C is correct. The Fox bragged to the Cat that he had several ways of escaping his enemy. The Cat only knew one way of escape and used it. The Fox wasted too much time trying to decide which method of escape he should choose and ended up getting caught. Answer choices A, B, and D are not themes of this story.
7.	A	Answer choice A is correct. Had the man offered to share his chicken, it would not have turned into a toad forever requiring attention. Answer choices B, C and D are incorrect because none of them are themes of this story.
8.	A	Answer choice A is correct. The theme is implicitly stated. That is, the reader must use the actions of the man, hiding the roasted chicken so he doesn't have to share, to determine the theme of the text. Answer choices B, C and D are incorrect because they are not reasonable.

© Lumos Information Services 2016 | LumosLearning.com

Question	Answer	Detailed Explanation
9.	B	Answer choice B is correct. The Crow learns that she should not be so trusting of someone who lavishes her with compliments. Considered universally, the theme then becomes don't be trusting of flatterers. Answer choices A, C and D are not themes of this story.
10.	C	Answer choice C is correct. The narrator volunteered to lead the walk-a-thon primarily to get Abbie off Katrina's back. Her intentions were not pure - she did not volunteer in order to help the class earn money for their graduation party. Answer choices A, B, and D are incorrect because they are not themes of the passage. They are not lessons the main character learned that can be applied universally.

Lesson 4: Objective Summary (RL.8.2)

Question	Answer	Detailed Explanation
1.	B	Answer choice B is correct. An objective summary is one that does not include an opinion. Answer choices A, C, and D are not definitions of an objective summary.
2.	B	Answer choice B is correct. Objective summaries should always be brief, accurate, and objective. Additionally, they should not include details from the text. Answer choices A, C, and D do not describe the attributes of a good objective summary.
3.	B	Answer choice B is correct. An objective summary should adequately summarize the text. Answer choice A is incorrect because an objective summary should not include opinions. Answer choice C is incorrect because a summary should not include information about all the characters in a text. Answer choice D is incorrect because a summary does not have a specific length.
4.	A	Answer choice A is correct. It is brief, accurate and objective. Answer choice B is incorrect as it is not objective or accurate. Answer choice C is incorrect as it does not contain enough information. Answer choice D is incorrect because it is not accurate or objective.
5.	B	Answer choice B is correct. Answer choices A, C, and D are incorrect as they do not summarize the passage accurately or objectively.
6.	B	Answer choice B is correct. This sentence summarizes the key points of the speech in a brief, accurate and objective manner. Answer choice A is incorrect because it contains too much information. Answer choice C is incorrect because it does not contain enough specific information. Answer choice D is incorrect because it is not objective.
7.	C	Answer choice C is correct. This summary includes the opinion of the writer. Nothing in the speech indicates that Lincoln was stressed. Answer choice A is incorrect because a summary is never copied word for word. Answer choice B is incorrect because the summary is not objective.

Question	Answer	Detailed Explanation
8.	B	Answer choice B is correct. It does not include any opinion and summarize Hook's personality, not his appearance. Answer choice A is incorrect because it summarizes Hook's appearance, not his personality. Answer choice C is incorrect because it is an opinion and does not include a summary of the text. Answer choice D is incorrect because it includes an opinion, "James Hook was a scary man."
9.	C	Answer choice C is correct. The summary provided simply paraphrases, or mixes up the words in the passage. Summaries must be original and not paraphrased. Answer choice A is incorrect because the summary is objective. Answer choice B is incorrect because the summary is not perfect. Answer choice D is incorrect because the information contained within the summary is correct. Remember, though, a summary should not be paraphrased.
10.	D	Answer choice D is correct. The summary is brief, accurate, and objective. Answer choice A is incorrect because it does not include enough information. Answer choice B is incorrect because it is not objective. Answer choice C is incorrect because it is not accurate.

© Lumos Information Services 2016 | LumosLearning.com

Lesson 5: Plot (RL.8.2)

Question	Answer	Detailed Explanation
1.	C	Answer choice C is correct. There are five elements of a plot. They are the introduction (sometimes identified as the exposition), rising action, climax, falling action, and resolution. Answer choices A, B, and D are incorrect.
2.	A	Answer choice A is correct. The two types of conflict are internal and external. Internal conflict is when the struggle is between the character and himself. External conflict is when an outside force causes the conflict. Answer choices B, C, and D are incorrect.
3.	B	Answer choice B is correct. The plot of the story is the series of events in the story. Answer choices A, C, and D are incorrect.
4.	A	Answer choice A is correct. The conflict is that there is not enough money for a graduation party. This conflict is man vs fate because the students had not direct control. There are other conflicts in the story, but the major conflict is the lack of money. Answer choices B, C, and D are incorrect.
5.	A	Answer choice A is correct. The conflict in the story is that there is not enough money for 8th grade graduation party. It is worth noting that the reader learns of the conflict in the introduction of the story. Answer choices B, C, and D are incorrect.
6.	D	Answer choice D is correct. The introduction or exposition is where the reader is introduced to the character, setting, and conflict. The exposition occurs at the beginning of the story. Answer choices A, B, and C are incorrect as they are not part of the introduction or exposition of the story.
7.	A	Answer choice A is correct. There are other events that occur in the rising action of the story, but the narrator volunteering to take charge of the walk-a-thon is the most important event as everything that comes next in the story is related to that action. Answer choices B, C, and D are not important events in the rising action of the story.
8.	C	Answer choice C is correct. The climax is the turning point, and the narrator's confession is the turning point. The reader doesn't know if the principal will let the students keep the money or make them return it. Answer choices A, B, and D are not the climax of the story.

© Lumos Information Services 2016 | LumosLearning.com

Question	Answer	Detailed Explanation
9.	A	Answer choice A is correct. The most important event in the falling action is when the narrator learns she must contact all the donors and tell them the truth about what their donations were funding. Answer choices B, C, and D are not part of the falling action of this story.
10.	C	Answer choice C is correct. The resolution of the story occurs when the narrator learns the principal will not allow the money earned to be used for a graduation party. Remember the resolution is the part of the story where the conflict is resolved. In this case, the conflict is that there is not money for a graduation party. The resolution to the conflict is that there will be no graduation party. Not all conflicts have a happy resolution. Answer choices A, B, and D are not resolutions to the story.

Lesson 6: Setting (RL. 8.2)

Question	Answer	Detailed Explanation
1.	A	Answer choice A is correct. The setting is usually introduced in the introduction or exposition. Note: the setting may change throughout the course of the story. Answer choices B, C, and D are incorrect as the setting is usually introduced in the introduction or exposition of the story.
2.	A	Answer choice A is correct. Stories can have more than one setting as the characters move through the story. Answer choice B, C, and D are incorrect.
3.	C	Answer choice C is correct. The setting of a story can be relayed through the culture of the characters. Answer choices A, B, and D are incorrect.
4.	B	Answer choice B is correct. The setting of the story tells the reader the time and place of action in the story. Answer choices A, C, and D are not part of the setting in the story.
5.	D	Answer choice D is correct. The mood of the main character, also known as the protagonist, cannot help the reader to determine the setting. However, the time of day, weather, and time of year all help to contribute to the setting.
6.	A	Answer choice A is correct. Clues to help the reader understand the setting is in an airport include Lauren waiting at the arrival gate and the reference to eleven hours in the air. Answer choices B, C and D are incorrect.
7.	D	Answer choice D is correct. There is not enough information to determine the setting of this excerpt as it is a description of a character. Answer choices A, B and C are incorrect as the setting cannot be determined from the information provided.
8.	A	Answer choice A is correct. Charlie is still at his home in Texas. A clue to help the reader understand the setting is in Texas is in the last sentence of the first paragraph, "Before he left..." This information leads the reader to understand that Charlie is still at home in Texas, and his mother is going to show him how to do the laundry before he leaves for school in New York. Answer choices B and C are incorrect because there are no clues to lead the reader to conclude either location is the first setting. Answer choice D is incorrect because there is information that helps determine the setting.

© Lumos Information Services 2016 | LumosLearning.com

Question	Answer	Detailed Explanation
9.	C	Answer choice C is correct. The description of the narrator's mother does not help the reader determine the setting. Answer choices A, B, and D are correct as they all help the reader determine the setting.
10.	C	Answer choice C is correct. The setting is where the fossils were found which is by a canal near the Guadalupe River in the Silicon Valley. Answer choice A is incorrect as the setting is not in Columbia. Answer choice B is incorrect. The scientists working with the fossils are from The University of California Berkeley. Answer choice D is incorrect because the reader is able to determine the setting.

Lesson 7: Characters (RL . 8.2)

Question	Answer	Detailed Explanation
1.	A	Answer choice A is correct. A round character is one who has many personality traits and is rather complex. Round characters tend to be more involved in the story. Answer choices B, C, and D are incorrect.
2.	A	Answer choice A is correct. The protagonist of a story is the main character. This character is who propels the story forward. Answer choices B, C, and D are incorrect.
3.	B	Answer choice B is correct. The antagonist of a story is opposing force to the main character or protagonist. The antagonist is not always a character. It may be fate or something in nature. Answer choices A, C, and D are incorrect.
4.	B	Answer choice B is correct. A static character does not experience any sort of change during the course of a story. Answer choices A, C, and D are incorrect.
5.	A	Answer choice A is correct. A dynamic character is one who changes during the course of the story due to the events that occur in the story. Answer choices B, C, and D are incorrect.
6.	A	Answer choice A is the correct answer. The narrator is the major character in the story because she is the most important character and propels the story forward. The narrator is also the protagonist. Answer choices B, C and D are incorrect.
7.	A	Answer choice A is correct. Dickens uses indirect characterization to describe the character of Scrooge. Through Scrooge's comments, the reader learns of Scrooge's personality traits. In the first excerpt, the reader learns through Scrooge's commentary that he is penny-pinching and crochety. In the second excerpt, the reader learns through Scrooge's commentary that he is happy and generous. Answer choice B is incorrect because the author does not describe the character of Scrooge to the reader. Answer choices C and D are also incorrect.

© Lumos Information Services 2016 | LumosLearning.com

Question	Answer	Detailed Explanation
8.	D	Answer choice D is correct. The character of Scrooge (the uncle) is dynamic. He undergoes a change from the beginning to the end of the book. At the beginning of the book, Stave One, he is a selfish, penny-pincher not willing to even wish a Merry Christmas to his nephew. At the end of the book, Stave Five, Scrooge undergoes a dramatic change and is now not only willing to wish even a stranger on the street a Merry Christmas, but he's also willing to part with his hard earned money. Answer choices A, B, are incorrect. Answer choice C is incorrect because we do not have enough of the story to determine if Scrooge's character is round. It is worth noting, however, that dynamic characters are usually round.
9.	A	Answer choice A is correct. The author tells the reader about Captain Carter. The reader does not have to make any inferences or guesses about his personality based on what he says or does or what others say about him. Answer choice B is incorrect because indirect characterization means the reader must make inferences about the character based on his actions, comments, or others statements about him. Answer choice C and D are not valid choices.
10.	C	Answer choice C is correct. Captain Carter is a round character. His personality traits are complex, and he seems to be a realistic character. Answer choice A is incorrect because a flat character would not have many personality traits. Answer choice B is incorrect because a static character is one who doesn't change during the course of a story. Flat characters are generally considered static. Answer choices D is incorrect simply because we do not have enough of the story to see a change in Captain Carter. Generally, dynamic characters are considered round.

© Lumos Information Services 2016 | LumosLearning.com

Lesson 8: Analyzing Literature (RL.8.3)

Question	Answer	Detailed Explanation
1.	A	Answer choice A is correct. Because of Charlie's reaction to his shrunken, miscolored clothes, it is evident he doesn't overreact when faced with obstacles but works to find solutions. Answer choices B, C, and D are incorrect.
2.	A	Answer choice A is correct. The plot of the story builds on Charlie's parents' expectations. When his mom gives him instructions on doing laundry, she expects he will listen and follow those instructions. Answer choices B, C, and D are incorrect.
3.	B	Answer choice B is correct. Dickens (the author) includes this dialogue so the reader completely understands Scrooge's change in attitude toward Chrismas during the story. Answer choices A, C, and D are incorrect.
4.	A	Answer choice A is correct. This dialogue is important because it allows the reader to see the change Scrooge underwent throughout the course of the story. Readers can learn much about characters through their dialogue. Answer choices B, C, and D are incorrect.
5.	D	Answer choice D is correct. When readers are asked what characters' actions reveal, they are essentially being asked to analyze how a character's actions and interactions with the plot, setting, and other characters will move the story forward.
6.	B	Answer choice B is correct. Casey Jones was a courageous man who was concerned about getting his train to its destination on time. Casey did not expect to see another train stalled on the tracks; therefore, he was not prepared to stop. As his last act of courage, Casey warned anyone nearby of impending doom by blowing the whistle and trying to stop the train. Answer choices A, C, and D are incorrect.
7.	C	Answer choice C is correct. As the train rounded the corner, Casey could see disaster ahead and warned the firemen. This is the act of a courageous man. Answer choices A, B, and D are incorrect.
8.	A	Answer choice A is correct. The ant is too busy to stop working and instead carries the kernel while explaining what he is doing to the grasshopper. The ant knows that he must continue with the work in order to be prepared for the upcoming winter. Answer choices B, C, and D are incorrect.

© Lumos Information Services 2016 | LumosLearning.com

Question	Answer	Detailed Explanation
9.	C	Answer choice C is correct. The grasshopper is irresponsible as he is more interested in singing than planning for the future. Answer choices A, B, and D are incorrect.
10.	D	Answer choice D is correct. The ants were working so hard to prepare for the winter; they found it hard to believe that not everyone did the same. Answer choices A, B, and C are incorrect.

Lesson 9: Meaning and Tone (RL.8.4)

Question	Answer	Detailed Explanation
1.	C	Answer choice C is correct. Tone tells the reader the way the author feels about the topic. Tone can be sad, excited, angry, and humorous - really, just about any emotion. Tone is expressed through word choice or phrasing and sometimes uses figurative language. One way to determine the tone of a piece of writing is to ask yourself how the author feels about the topic he or she has written. Answer choices A, B and D are incorrect.
2.	A	Answer choice A is correct. The statement about tone is neutral or indifferent, meaning the writer did not include any language that relays his or her attitude toward the homework assignment. It is just a statement of fact. Answer choice B, C and D are incorrect because the correct tone is neutral.
3.	C	Answer choice C is correct. The author's tone is sarcastic which inspires a slightly humorous atmosphere although he is clearly unhappy about the assignment. Answer choices A, B, and D are incorrect.
4.	A	Answer choice A is correct. The author is angry about the homework assignment. When determining tone, ask yourself how the author feels and what words he or she uses to convey his feelings. Answer choices B, C, and D are incorrect.
5.	C	Answer choice C is correct. The tone of the excerpt is enthusiastic. DiCamillo wants the reader to feel excited while reading this passage. Answer choices A, B, and D are incorrect.
6.	A	Answer choice A is correct. The tone is hopeful and encouraging. Pay close attention to the word choice: turning point, rekindled, revived. These are all words that convey a sense of encouragement. Answer choices B, C and D are incorrect.
7.	D	Answer choice D is correct. The tone is comical as Hoffmann describes the bumbling huntsman and hiding hare. Answer choices A, B, and C are incorrect.
8.	B	Answer choice B is correct. The hare is hiding from the huntsman in the leaves and grass. He is not noticed as the huntsman walks past because he is snug or fitting closely in the leaves and grass. Answer choices A, C, and D are incorrect.

© Lumos Information Services 2016 | LumosLearning.com

Question	Answer	Detailed Explanation
9.	D	Answer choice D is correct. In this excerpt, "spectacles" most closely means glasses. The huntsman realizes he cannot see to hunt without his spectacles or glasses. Humorously, even with his spectacles, or glasses, perched upon his nose, he still does not see the hare hiding. Answer choices A, B, and C are incorrect.
10.	A	Answer choice A is correct. The ungrateful son does not want to share the chicken with his father so he hastily, or quickly, hides it. Decisions made in haste can often end up being poor decisions. Hasty decisions are quick and done without much thought. Answer choices B, C, and D are incorrect.

Lesson 10: Compare and Contrast (RL.8.5)

Question	Answer	Detailed Explanation
1.	A	The correct answer is A. When you are comparing, you are looking for similarities. When looking at two pieces of text, if you are asked to compare them, you are being asked to look for what is similar within the two pieces of text. Answer choices B, C, and D are incorrect.
2.	C	Answer choice C is correct. A paper or article that is comparing two things will likely use signal words such as likewise, as well, the same as, both, similarly, or too. These are not the only signal words, but they are quite common. Answer choices A, B, and D are incorrect.
3.	A	Answer choice A is correct. A Venn diagram provides space for both comparing (the center where the circle meet) and contrasting (the outer circles). Answer choices B, C, and D are incorrect.
4.	B	The correct answer is B. When you are contrasting, you are looking for differences. When you are looking at two pieces of text, if you are asked about contrasts, you are being asked to tell the difference between the two pieces of text. Answer choices A, C, and D are incorrect.
5.	A	The correct answer is A. Common information in a Venn diagram goes in the middles where the two circles intersect. Contrasting information goes in the outer portions of the circle. Answer choices B, C, and D are incorrect.
6.	D	Answer choice D is correct. A paper or article that is contrasting two things will likely use signal words such as although, however, contrary to, unlike, and unless. These are not the only signal words, but they are quite common. Answer choices A, B, and C are incorrect.
7.	D	Answer choice D is correct. All three statements reflect differences, or contrasts, in the text.
8.	A	Answer choice A is correct. The eagle is a confident flyer, but the seagull is afraid to leave the ledge. Answer choices B, C, and D are incorrect.

© Lumos Information Services 2016 | LumosLearning.com

Question	Answer	Detailed Explanation
9.	B	Answer choice B is correct. Neither passage discusses the process of flying.
10.	C	Answer choice C is correct. This question is asking the reader to make a comparison - what does flying enable BOTH birds to do. The word BOTH is key because it tells the reader to compare the birds from each passage. Flying enables both birds to find food to eat. Answer choices A, B, and D are incorrect.

Lesson 11: Producing Suspense and Humor (RL.8.6)

Question	Answer	Detailed Explanation
1.	D	Answer choice D is correct. All of the choices are puns.
2.	D	Answer choice D is correct. Irony, puns, setting and situation can all add humor to a story.
3.	C	Answer choice C is correct. Irony is a surprising funny, or interesting contradiction. It is a situation that occurs which is the opposite of what is expected to occur. Answer choices A, B, and D are incorrect.
4.	A	Answer choice A is correct. The author creates humor by creating a rabbit that is amused by the bumbling hunter who passes right by him. Answer choices B, C, and D are incorrect.
5.	B	Answer choice B is correct. The author builds suspense by setting up a mood of apprehension and including foreshadowing. Answer choices A, C, and D are incorrect.
6.	A	Answer choice A is correct. Dramatic irony is used because the reader knows something that the character of Romeo does not know. Believing his beloved is dead, he kills himself. Answer choices B, C, and D are incorrect.
7.	B	Answer choice B is correct. Verbal irony is used because the man says he is happy he woke up early to wash his car, but in reality his efforts were futile since his car is now dirty. He did not sincerely mean what he said. Answer choices A, C, and D are incorrect.
8.	C	Answer choice C is correct. Situational irony is used because the reader expects the rehabilitated seals will swim off into the ocean and live happily ever after. Answer choices A, B, and D are incorrect.

Question	Answer	Detailed Explanation
9.	A	Answer choice A is correct. Situational irony is used by the author. After saving for years for a dream vacation, one suddenly appears in Caitlin's life. Answer choices B, C, and D are incorrect.
10.	B	Answer choice B is correct. The author uses verbal irony as Kyle's mother doesn't really believe that beating the next level in the video game is important. She is making a point that studying is more important than playing games. Answer choices A, C, and D are incorrect.

Lesson 12: Media and Literature (RL.8.7)

Question	Answer	Detailed Explanation
1.	A	Answer choice A is correct because a video allows people to see a visualization.
2.	C	Answer choice C is correct. Media can aide an audience seeing and hearing.
3.	A	Answer choice A is correct. Since the question is asking for a visual interpretation, a movie will show viewers the interpretation of the director.
4.	B	Answer choice B is correct. The definition of multimedia is using more than one medium of expression or communication.
5.	C	Answer choice C is correct because it can be done quickly. While options A and B allow publication, a blog can be posted quickly.
6.	B	Answer choice B is correct because newspapers articles report the facts, while anyone can publish a blog.
7.	A	Answer choice A is correct because the image is only of the lake. The poem speaks of the lake, but it speaks more of the boy's memories associated with the lake.
8.	B	Answer choice B is correct because the poem talks about both sounds and sights.
9.	B	Answer choice B is correct because the question asks about both the lake and its surroundings. The image only shows the lake.
10.	A	Answer choice A is correct because the poem is about the author's personal cabin at the lake; therefore, it's not a travel destination while the image is of the entire lake and therefore open to the public.

© Lumos Information Services 2016 | LumosLearning.com

Lesson 13: Modern Fictions and Traditional Stories (RL.8.9)

Question	Answer	Detailed Explanation
1.	D	Answer choice D is correct. A motif is an element or idea in a story that recurs in traditional stories. Motifs can be characters, places, objects, actions or even style.
2.	D	Answer choice D is correct. While these are not all the motifs found in traditional stories, they encompass the majority of those stories. Consider the books and stories you read now. Can you find motifs in those that are similar to the motifs in traditional stories? If so, chances are what you are reading is a modern day retelling of a traditional story.
3.	C	Answer choice C is correct. The lesson, or moral, of the story is to work hard and prepare for the future. The grasshopper chose to play while the ants worked hard to gather food for the upcoming winter. Once the cold arrived, the grasshopper had nothing to eat, while the ants had plenty because they prepared.
4.	B	Answer choice B is correct. "The Ant and the Grasshopper" is a fable. It is thought to have originated from Aesop who lived over 2000 years ago. He was a storyteller and many fables are attributed to him.
5.	D	Answer choice D is correct. "The Ant and the Grasshopper" is a fable. Readers can recognize fables by their length, animal characters and lesson.
6.	A	Answer choice A is correct. Modern day Cinderellas are people who overcome odds and become successful.
7.	B	Answer choice B is correct. This story is a loose retelling of the fairy tale, "Goldilocks and the Three Bears" by Robert Southey. Traditional stories are often times retold into modern versions, thus the story lives on and is more applicable to modern times.
8.	B	Answer choice B is correct. The popular motif in this short story is a test of courage (character's actions). This is a loose adaptation of the classic fairy tale "Cinderella".

Question	Answer	Detailed Explanation
9.	B	Answer choice B is correct. Remember that fairy tales always include a good character and an evil character. In "Cinderella," Cinderella is the good character and her step-mother is evil, thus their characters represent good vs. evil.
10.	D	Answer choice D is correct. Casey Jones is a folktale that originated in Tennessee. Remember folktales were passed on by word of mouth. This entertaining version may differ from other versions you have heard or read.

© Lumos Information Services 2016 | LumosLearning.com

Reading: Informational Text
Key Ideas and Details

Lesson 1: Making Inferences Based on Textual Evidence (RI.8.1)

1.   What is an inference?

Ⓐ   an answer that is clearly stated in the text
Ⓑ   a logical conclusion drawn from evidence in a text
Ⓒ   an opinion made from reading a text
Ⓓ   a direct quotation found in the text

2.   What is the proper way to make a direct citation from a text?

Ⓐ   put the citation in italics
Ⓑ   underline the citation
Ⓒ   put the citation in quotes
Ⓓ   make the citation bold

3.   What is the best way to cite evidence from a text?

Ⓐ   summarize
Ⓑ   paraphrase
Ⓒ   in quotes
Ⓓ   all of the above

Stephen and Joseph Montgolfier were papermakers, but they had been interested in flying for many years. One night, in 1782, Joseph noticed something that gave him an idea. He was sitting in front of the fire when he saw some small pieces of scorched paper being carried up the chimney.

Soon afterwards, the brothers conducted an experiment. They lit a fire under a small silk bag, which was open at the bottom; at once, the bag rose to the ceiling. After this, Stephen and Joseph conducted many more experiments, both indoors and in the open air. Eventually, they built a huge balloon of linen and paper. On June 5th, 1783, they launched their balloon in the village of Annonay.

4.   What evidence in the passage shows that the Montgolfier brothers discovered how to make a hot air balloon?

Ⓐ   "He was sitting in front of the fire when he saw some small pieces of scorched paper being carried up the chimney."

Ⓑ   "Eventually, they built a huge balloon of linen and paper. On June 5th, 1783, they launched their balloon in the village of Annonay."

Ⓒ   "After this, Stephen and Joseph conducted many more experiments, both indoors and in the open air."

Ⓓ   none of the above

5.   What evidence in the text shows that the Montgolfier brothers launched the first successful hot air balloon?

Ⓐ   "He was sitting in front of the fire when he saw some small pieces of scorched paper being carried up the chimney."

Ⓑ   "Eventually, they built a huge balloon of linen and paper. On June 5th, 1783, they launched their balloon in the village of Annonay."

Ⓒ   "After this, Stephen and Joseph conducted many more experiments, both indoors and in the open air."

Ⓓ   none of the above

6.   What evidence in the text could lead you to infer that the Montgolfier brothers' experienced some trial and error before successfully launching a hot air balloon?

Ⓐ   "He was sitting in front of the fire when he saw some small pieces of scorched paper being carried up the chimney."

Ⓑ   "Eventually, they built a huge balloon of linen and paper. On June 5th, 1783, they launched their balloon in the village of Annonay."

Ⓒ   "After this, Stephen and Joseph conducted many more experiments, both indoors and in the open air."

Ⓓ   none of the above

© Lumos Information Services 2016 | LumosLearning.com

The Emperor Penguin is the only penguin species that breeds during the Antarctic winter. It treks 31–75 miles over the ice to breeding colonies, which may include thousands of penguins. The female lays a single egg, which is then incubated by the male while the female returns to the sea to feed; parents subsequently take turns foraging at sea and caring for their chick in the colony. The average lifespan of the Empire Penguin is 20 years, although observations suggest that some Emperor Penguins may live to 50 years of age.

7.   **What evidence in the text could lead you to infer both the male and female penguin share equally in the responsibility of raising the chick?**

   Ⓐ "The average lifespan of the Empire Penguin is 20 years,"
   Ⓑ "The Emperor Penguin is the only penguin species that breeds during the Antarctic winter."
   Ⓒ "...parents subsequently take turns foraging at sea and caring for their chick in the colony."
   Ⓓ "...some Emperor Penguins may live to 50 years of age."

8.   **What evidence in the text tells you what the penguins do to survive in the colony after the chick is born?**

   Ⓐ "The average lifespan of the Empire Penguin is 20 years,"
   Ⓑ "The Emperor Penguin is the only penguin species that breeds during the Antarctic winter."
   Ⓒ "...parents subsequently take turns foraging at sea and caring for their chick in the colon."
   Ⓓ "...some Emperor Penguins may live to 50 years of age."

© Lumos Information Services 2016 | LumosLearning.com

Excerpt from the Foreword of *A Princess of Mars* by Edgar Rice Burroughs

My first recollection of Captain Carter is of the few months he spent at my father's home in Virginia, just prior to the opening of the Civil War. I was then a child of but five years, yet I well remember the tall, dark, smooth-faced, athletic man whom I called Uncle Jack.

He seemed always to be laughing; and he entered into the sports of the children with the same hearty good fellowship he displayed toward those pastimes in which the men and women of his own age indulged; or he would sit for an hour at a time entertaining my old grandmother with stories of his strange wild life in all parts of the world. We all loved him, and our slaves fairly worshipped the ground he trod.

He was a splendid specimen of manhood, standing a good two inches over six feet, broad of shoulder and narrow of hip, with the carriage of the trained fighting man. His features were regular and clear cut, his hair black and closely cropped, while his eyes were of a steel gray, reflecting a strong and loyal character, filled with fire and initiative. His manners were perfect, and his courtliness was that of a typical southern gentleman of the highest type.

9. **Based on the evidence in the text, what can you determine about Captain Carter's personality?**

    Ⓐ   He was a happy man.
    Ⓑ   He was a hard worker.
    Ⓒ   He was ready to go to war.
    Ⓓ   He was a friendly man.

10. **Based on the evidence in the text what historical event is about to happen?**

    Ⓐ   World War II
    Ⓑ   World War I
    Ⓒ   Civil War
    Ⓓ   The Revolutionary war

© Lumos Information Services 2016 | LumosLearning.com

Lesson 2: Central Ideas (RI.8.2)

1. **What is a central idea?**

   Ⓐ the idea stated in the topic sentence
   Ⓑ the theme of a piece of literature
   Ⓒ who a piece of informational text is mainly about
   Ⓓ the main idea of a piece of informational text

2. **In what type of work do readers find central idea?**

   Ⓐ newspaper
   Ⓑ journal
   Ⓒ text book
   Ⓓ all of the above

3. **What statement is true about central idea?**

   Ⓐ It can sometimes be found in the title of the text.
   Ⓑ It is supported by the details in the text.
   Ⓒ It covers the whole text.
   Ⓓ all of the above

4. **When determining the central idea of a text, it is important not to confuse it with _____.**

   Ⓐ the topic
   Ⓑ the details
   Ⓒ none of the above
   Ⓓ both A & B

Stephen and Joseph Montgolfier were papermakers, but they had been interested in flying for many years. One night, in 1782, Joseph noticed something that gave him an idea. He was sitting in front of the fire when he saw some small pieces of scorched paper being carried up the chimney.

Soon afterwards, the brothers conducted an experiment. They lit a fire under a small silk bag, which was open at the bottom; at once, the bag rose to the ceiling. After this, Stephen and Joseph conducted many more experiments, both indoors and in the open air. Eventually, they built a huge balloon of linen and paper. On June 5th, 1783, they launched their balloon in the village of Annonay.

5.   What is the central idea of this passage?

   Ⓐ   The Montgolfier brothers were papermakers who became famous.
   Ⓑ   The Montgolfier brothers theorized that hot air can be used to propel a balloon into the air.
   Ⓒ   The Montgolfier brothers lost their jobs as papermakers because they were obsessed with their balloon.
   Ⓓ   The Montgolfier brothers liked to experiment.

The Emperor Penguin is the only penguin species that breeds during the Antarctic winter. It treks 31–75 miles over the ice to breeding colonies, which may include thousands of penguins. The female lays a single egg, which is then incubated by the male while the female returns to the sea to feed; parents subsequently take turns foraging at sea and caring for their chick in the colony. The average lifespan of the Empire Penguin is 20 years, although observations suggest that some Emperor Penguins may live to 50 years of age.

6.   What is the central idea of this passage?

   Ⓐ   The movie, Happy Feet was inspired by Emperor Penguins.
   Ⓑ   The male Emperor Penguin sits on the egg while the mother hunts for food.
   Ⓒ   Female Emperor penguins lay their eggs in the Antarctic and both male and female take turns caring for the egg until it hatches.
   Ⓓ   Emperor Penguins live over 50 years.

Archaeology is the study of past human life and culture through systematically examining and interpreting the material remains left behind. These material remains include archaeological sites (e.g. settlements, building features, graves), as well as cultural materials or artifacts such as tools and pottery. Through the interpretation and classification of archaeological materials, archaeologists work to understand past human behavior. In some countries, archaeology is often historical or art historical, with a strong emphasis on Culture history, archaeological sites, and artifacts such as art objects. In the New World, archaeology can be either a part of history and classical studies or anthropology.

The exact origins of archaeology as a discipline are uncertain. Excavations of ancient monuments and the collection of antiquities have been taking place for thousands of years. It was only in the 19th century, however, that the systematic study of the past through its physical remains began to be carried out in a manner recognizable to modern students of archaeology.

7.   **What is the central idea of this passage?**

   Ⓐ   the study of the origin of archaeology
   Ⓑ   the study of archaeology
   Ⓒ   the study of modern archaeology and anthropology
   Ⓓ   the study of the human past

8.   **What does the passage suggest about archaeologists?**

   Ⓐ   They study past human life and culture by examining materials left by early humans.
   Ⓑ   They study humans and their interaction with their surroundings.
   Ⓒ   They study humans and their families by looking at the things they left behind.
   Ⓓ   They study art history.

Quinoa is a grain like seed. It is considered a whole grain and is cooked in much the same way as rice. Quinoa has many health benefits including nine essential amino acids and is cholesterol free. Additionally quinoa is gluten-free and kosher. Quinoa is a good source of protein and easily digestible.

9.   **What is the central idea of the passage above?**

   Ⓐ   the health benefits of quinoa
   Ⓑ   how to cook quinoa
   Ⓒ   why people should eat quinoa
   Ⓓ   why people should cook quinoa

Cooking quinoa is much like cooking rice. Depending on the sort of quinoa you purchase, you may have to rinse the seed-like spores before cooking. Be sure to check the label. Boil two cups of water, vegetable stock, chicken broth or other liquid of your choice. Add one cup of raw (rinsed if necessary) quinoa and simmer for about twenty minutes. It doesn't take long for quinoa to cook up moist and tender.

10.   What is the central idea of this passage?

Ⓐ   the health benefits of quinoa

Ⓑ   how to cook quinoa

Ⓒ   quinoa as a meat replacement

Ⓓ   none of the above

Lesson 3: Connections and Distinctions (RI.8.3)

1.   What does it mean to make a distinction?

   Ⓐ to find a similarity
   Ⓑ to find a difference
   Ⓒ to draw a conclusion
   Ⓓ to point out a fact

2.   What does it mean to make a connection?

   Ⓐ to find a similarity
   Ⓑ to find a difference
   Ⓒ to draw a conclusion
   Ⓓ to point out a fact

3.   What is similar between New World archeology and archeology of the past?

   Ⓐ They both focus on history.
   Ⓑ They both focus on art.
   Ⓒ They both focus on culture.
   Ⓓ all of the above

4.   Based on the information in the article, where would a good place to examine archaeology be?

   Ⓐ online
   Ⓑ at a museum
   Ⓒ in a book
   Ⓓ all of the above

Cooking quinoa is much like cooking rice. Depending on the sort of quinoa you purchase, you may have to rinse the seed-like spores before cooking. Be sure to check the label. Boil two cups of water, vegetable stock, chicken broth or other liquid of your choice. Add one cup of raw (rinsed if necessary) quinoa and simmer for about twenty minutes. It doesn't take long for quinoa to cook up moist and tender.

5.   What is one distinction that the passage reminds you to take?

Ⓐ   They type of quinoa you buy will determine if you have to rinse.

Ⓑ   There are different types of quinoa that taste differently.

Ⓒ   Always feel the quinoa before buying it.

Ⓓ   The type of liquid to use is your choice.

Marathon

Training for a marathon takes hard work and perseverance. It is not something you can do on the spur of the moment. Preparing for a marathon takes months, particularly if you have never run a marathon before. The official distance of a full marathon is 26.2 miles. In 2005, the average time to complete a marathon in the United States was 4 hours 32 minutes 8 seconds for men and 5 hours 6 minutes 8 seconds for women.

Most people who run marathons are not trying to win. Many runners try to beat their own best time. Some compare their time to other runners in the same gender and age group. Some people set time-oriented goals, such as finishing under four hours, while others try to complete the race without slowing to a walk. Many beginners simply hope to finish the marathon.

Trainers recommend that beginners maintain a consistent running schedule for six weeks prior to even starting a marathon training program. The purpose of this is to allow the body to adapt to the various physical demands of long distance running. First-time marathon runners should train by running four days a week for at least four months, increasing distance by no more than ten percent weekly. As race day approaches, runners should taper their runs, reducing the strain on their bodies and resting before the marathon. It is important not to over exert yourself during training because that can lead to lot of injuries. Most common injuries are spraining of the knees and ankles. These sprains can hinder the training.

Before the race, it is important to stretch in order to keep muscles limber. Staying hydrated is also important, but there is a danger in drinking too much water. If a runner drinks too much water, they may experience a dangerous condition called hyponatremia, a drop of sodium levels in the blood. So only drink water when you are thirsty. During the race, trainers recommend maintaining a steady pace. It is normal to feel sore after a marathon. Light exercise will help sore muscles heal faster.

© Lumos Information Services 2016 | LumosLearning.com

Some people run marathons in pairs or groups. Training for and running a marathon with another person or group of people can make the experience more enjoyable and more rewarding. A running partner might be just the motivation you need to show up for an early morning run instead of rolling over to hit the snooze button. And, when you cross the finish line together, you can share the satisfaction of reaching your common goal.

Usually, thousands of people sign up and run a Marathon. Most people finish the race. The thrill of running a marathon for the first time is unbelievable. The training sessions are harder if you have never run before. But it is unbelievable what ones' body can do when one puts their mind to it. Having a good coach to support you makes all the difference in training for a marathon.

The daily runs are very important. Strength training and core training are also very important.

The health benefits you gain from training are tremendous. Your core muscles grow stronger, and you will have tighter thighs and gluts. Your heart will be much stronger, and you can maintain lower cholesterol and blood sugar levels. Over all, you will look better and become healthier.

Nothing can explain how people feel when they reach that finish line at the end of the race. All the hard work and months of training feel worthwhile. The feeling of accomplishing something great overtakes you. It is great to run a marathon, but it is even greater to finish it.

6.   How is a marathon competition different than most competitions?

Ⓐ   Runners compete against themselves to beat past times.

Ⓑ   Runners do not compete against each other.

Ⓒ   Runners set their own personal records.

Ⓓ   all of the above

7.   What makes marathon running similar to other competitive sports?

Ⓐ   health benefits

Ⓑ   trophies

Ⓒ   winning

Ⓓ   numbers of people

You read a research study that says eating a candy bar made of dark chocolate every day is good for your heart in the long run. The study followed the health of a large group of people over the course of ten years. You notice in fine print at the end of the research that the study was conducted by a major chocolate company.

8.   What connection can you make with this study and other commercials you see on TV?

Ⓐ   The study must be true if it is published.

Ⓑ   Advertising agencies sometimes minimize major facts to help sell products.

Ⓒ   Studies in all commercials are conducted by one research company.

Ⓓ   Dark chocolate is good for your heart.

From Chapter 1 of *Bullets and Billets* by Bruce Bainsfather

I stood in a queue of Gordons, Seaforths, Worcesters, etc., slowly moving up one, until, finally arriving at the companion (nearly said staircase), I tobogganed down into the hold, and spent what was left of the night dealing out those rations. Having finished at last, I came to the surface again, and now, as the transport glided along through the dirty waters of the river, and as I gazed at the motley collection of Frenchmen on the various wharves, and saw a variety of soldiery, and a host of other warlike "props," I felt acutely that now I was in the war at last—the real thing! For some time I had been rehearsing in England; but that was over now, and here I was—in the common or garden vernacular—"in the soup."

9.   Based on the context of the phrase "in the soup," what can you conclude the author is saying?

Ⓐ   He's happy he has reached his destination.

Ⓑ   He's hungry and ready to eat.

Ⓒ   He is entering a bad situation.

Ⓓ   He came to the surface and spent time.

10.   What conclusion can you draw about this passage?

Ⓐ   The narrator is heading into war.

Ⓑ   The narrator is going on a trip.

Ⓒ   The narrator is frustrated about his journey.

Ⓓ   The narrator likes rivers.

© Lumos Information Services 2016 | LumosLearning.com

Craft and Structure

Lesson 4: Determining Meaning of Words (RI.8.4)

1. **What is connotation?**

    Ⓐ   a dictionary definition
    Ⓑ   what a word means based on its context in a story
    Ⓒ   a word with multiple meanings
    Ⓓ   an opinion based on fact

2. **What is denotation?**

    Ⓐ   a dictionary definition
    Ⓑ   what a word means based on its context in a story
    Ⓒ   a word that has a meaning that has changed over time
    Ⓓ   an opinion based on fact

The Emperor Penguin is the only penguin species that breeds during the Antarctic winter. It treks 31–75 miles over the ice to breeding colonies, which may include thousands of penguins. The female lays a single egg, which is then incubated by the male while the female returns to the sea to feed; parents subsequently take turns foraging at sea and caring for their chick in the colony. The average lifespan of the Empire Penguin is 20 years, although observations suggest that some Emperor Penguins may live to 50 years of age.

3. **Based on how the word "trek" is used in the passage, determine its meaning.**

    Ⓐ   to fly a long distance
    Ⓑ   to circulate in a specific area
    Ⓒ   to walk a long distance
    Ⓓ   to live a long life

Archaeology is the study of past human life and culture through systematically examining and interpreting the material remains left behind. These material remains include archaeological sites (e.g. settlements, building features, graves), as well as cultural materials or artifacts such as tools and pottery. Through the interpretation and classification of archaeological materials, archaeologists work to understand past human behavior. In some countries, archaeology is often historical or art historical, with a strong emphasis on Culture history, archaeological sites, and artifacts such as art objects. In the New World, archaeology can be either a part of history and classical studies or anthropology.

The exact origins of archaeology as a discipline are uncertain. Excavations of ancient monuments and the collection of antiquities have been taking place for thousands of years. It was only in the 19th century, however, that the systematic study of the past through its physical remains began to be carried out in a manner recognizable to modern students of archaeology.

4.   What does the underlined word "professionalization" mean?

  Ⓐ   the way a field of study turns into a professional job
  Ⓑ   the way an artifact turns into a noted antique
  Ⓒ   the way a civilization is recovered and displayed
  Ⓓ   to study art history

5.   What does it mean to do something "systematically"?

  Ⓐ   to follow very specific instructions
  Ⓑ   to use the scientific method of trial and error
  Ⓒ   to record the process you followed to do something
  Ⓓ   none of the above

Marathon

Training for a marathon takes hard work and perseverance. It is not something you can do on the spur of the moment. Preparing for a marathon takes months, particularly if you have never run a marathon before. The official distance of a full marathon is 26.2 miles. In 2005, the average time to complete a marathon in the United States was 4 hours 32 minutes 8 seconds for men and 5 hours 6 minutes 8 seconds for women.

Most people who run marathons are not trying to win. Many runners try to beat their own best time. Some compare their time to other runners in the same gender and age group. Some people set time-oriented goals, such as finishing under four hours, while others try to complete the race without slowing to a walk. Many beginners simply hope to finish the marathon.

Trainers recommend that beginners maintain a consistent running schedule for six weeks prior to even starting a marathon training program. The purpose of this is to allow the body to adapt to the various physical demands of long distance running. First-time marathon runners should train by running four days a week for at least four months, increasing distance by no more than ten percent weekly. As race day approaches, runners should taper their runs, reducing the strain on their bodies and resting before the marathon. It is important not to over exert yourself during training because that can lead to lot of injuries. Most common injuries are spraining of the knees and ankles. These sprains can hinder the training.

Before the race, it is important to stretch in order to keep muscles limber. Staying hydrated is also important, but there is a danger in drinking too much water. If a runner drinks too much water, they may experience a dangerous condition called hyponatremia, a drop of sodium levels in the blood. So only drink water when you are thirsty. During the race, trainers recommend maintaining a steady pace. It is normal to feel sore after a marathon. Light exercise will help sore muscles heal faster.

Some people run marathons in pairs or groups. Training for and running a marathon with another person or group of people can make the experience more enjoyable and more rewarding. A running partner might be just the motivation you need to show up for an early morning run instead of rolling over to hit the snooze button. And, when you cross the finish line together, you can share the satisfaction of reaching your common goal.

Usually, thousands of people sign up and run a Marathon. Most people finish the race. The thrill of running a marathon for the first time is unbelievable. The training sessions are harder if you have never run before. But it is unbelievable what ones' body can do when one puts their mind to it. Having a good coach to support you makes all the difference in training for a marathon.

The daily runs are very important. Strength training and core training are also very important.

The health benefits you gain from training are tremendous. Your core muscles grow stronger, and you will have tighter thighs and gluts. Your heart will be much stronger, and you can maintain lower cholesterol and blood sugar levels. Over all, you will look better and become healthier.

Nothing can explain how people feel when they reach that finish line at the end of the race. All the hard work and months of training feel worthwhile. The feeling of accomplishing something great overtakes you. It is great to run a marathon, but it is even greater to finish it.

"Nothing can explain how people feel when they reach that finish line at the end of the race. All the hard work and months of training feel worthwhile."

6.   **What does the phrase "overexert" (third paragraph) mean?**

Ⓐ   go over the amount of time you need to run
Ⓑ   go over the distance you need to run
Ⓒ   do more than your body can handle
Ⓓ   drink too much water

Name: _____   Date: _____

7. **What does the phrase "spur of the moment" (first paragraph) mean?**

    Ⓐ in the moment, without thinking
    Ⓑ at the last minute
    Ⓒ on a horse wearing spurs
    Ⓓ taking time to train

8. **How does the phrase "spur of the moment" add to the tone of the passage?**

    Ⓐ It creates a humorous tone so the readers laugh and enjoy the piece.
    Ⓑ It creates a serious tone necessary to show how hard running a marathon is.
    Ⓒ It creates a factual tone so readers can study before training.
    Ⓓ It creates a reminder of how important training is.

From Chapter 1 of *Bullets and Billets* by Bruce Bainsfather

I stood in a queue of Gordons, Seaforths, Worcesters, etc., slowly moving up one, until, finally arriving at the companion (nearly said staircase), I tobogganed down into the hold, and spent what was left of the night dealing out those rations. Having finished at last, I came to the surface again, and now, as the transport glided along through the dirty waters of the river, and as I gazed at the motley collection of Frenchmen on the various wharves, and saw a variety of soldiery, and a host of other warlike "props," I felt acutely that now I was in the war at last—the real thing! For some time I had been rehearsing in England; but that was over now, and here I was—in the common or garden vernacular—"in the soup."

9. **Based on how they are used to begin the passage, what are "Gordons, Seaforths, and Worcesters?**

    Ⓐ ranks in an army
    Ⓑ types of holding facilities on a ship
    Ⓒ different destinations on the journey
    Ⓓ none of the above

10. **The author is using what type of figurative language to compare war to a theater in the above passage.**

    Ⓐ implied metaphor
    Ⓑ simile
    Ⓒ imagery
    Ⓓ allusion

110
© Lumos Information Services 2016 | LumosLearning.com

Lesson 5: Analyzing Structures in Text (RI.8.5)

1. **What should you look at when analyzing the structure of a piece of text?**

   Ⓐ the genre of writing
   Ⓑ the author's purpose
   Ⓒ the types of transition words that are being used
   Ⓓ all of the above

2. **What type of writing has the following literary elements: characters, conflict, setting, and plot?**

   Ⓐ nonfiction
   Ⓑ fiction
   Ⓒ technical
   Ⓓ poetry

3. **If you saw words such as, "unlike", "as well as", "on the other hand", and "in contrast", what would you think the author's purpose was?**

   Ⓐ to persuade
   Ⓑ to compare
   Ⓒ to entertain
   Ⓓ wouldn't be able to tell

Stephen and Joseph Montgolfier were papermakers, but they had been interested in flying for many years. One night, in 1782, Joseph noticed something that gave him an idea. He was sitting in front of the fire when he saw some small pieces of scorched paper being carried up the chimney.

Soon afterwards, the brothers conducted an experiment. They lit a fire under a small silk bag, which was open at the bottom; at once, the bag rose to the ceiling. After this, Stephen and Joseph conducted many more experiments, both indoors and in the open air. Eventually, they built a huge balloon of linen and paper. On June 5th, 1783, they launched their balloon in the village of Annonay.

4. What would change this passage into an essay?

- Ⓐ adding an introductory paragraph and a conclusion
- Ⓑ adding more details to the experiments
- Ⓒ adding nothing, it is already an essay
- Ⓓ rewriting it as a personal narrative

5. What type of text structure is used in this passage?

- Ⓐ sequence
- Ⓑ compare/contrast
- Ⓒ cause/effect
- Ⓓ description

The Emperor Penguin is the only penguin species that breeds during the Antarctic winter. It treks 31–75 miles over the ice to breeding colonies, which may include thousands of penguins. The female lays a single egg, which is then incubated by the male while the female returns to the sea to feed; parents subsequently take turns foraging at sea and caring for their chick in the colony. The average lifespan of the Empire Penguin is 20 years, although observations suggest that some Emperor Penguins may live to 50 years of age.

6. What type of text structure is used in the passage above?

- Ⓐ sequence
- Ⓑ compare/contrast
- Ⓒ description
- Ⓓ cause/effect

Archaeology is the study of past human life and culture through systematically examining and interpreting the material remains left behind. These material remains include archaeological sites (e.g. settlements, building features, graves), as well as cultural materials or artifacts such as tools and pottery. Through the interpretation and classification of archaeological materials, archaeologists work to understand past human behavior. In some countries, archaeology is often historical or art historical, with a strong emphasis on Culture history, archaeological sites, and artifacts such as art objects. In the New World, archaeology can be either a part of history and classical studies or anthropology.

The exact origins of archaeology as a discipline are uncertain. Excavations of ancient monuments and the collection of antiquities have been taking place for thousands of years. It was only in the 19th century, however, that the systematic study of the past through its physical remains began to be carried out in a manner recognizable to modern students of archaeology.

"Archaeology is the study of past human life and culture through systematically examining and interpreting the material remains left behind."

7.   The author uses this as the opening line to his article in order to:

Ⓐ   give the reader a base to build their understanding of archaeology
Ⓑ   tell why archaeology is important
Ⓒ   give the reader an idea of what the article is going to be about
Ⓓ   both A and C

"Through the interpretation and classification of archaeological materials, archaeologists work to understand past human behavior."

8.   Why is this sentence included?

Ⓐ   to give an example of why archaeology is important
Ⓑ   to show the technical side of archaeology
Ⓒ   to show the process of archaeology
Ⓓ   to show how archaeology has changed

"Excavations of ancient monuments and the collection of antiquities have been taking place for thousands of years."

9.   Why was this sentence included?

Ⓐ   to clarify what archaeology is

Ⓑ   to show that archaeology is not something that was supported long ago

Ⓒ   to show that archaeology is a fairly modern concept

Ⓓ   to explain that some form of archaeology has been happening for a very long time

Marathon

Training for a marathon takes hard work and perseverance. It is not something you can do on the spur of the moment. Preparing for a marathon takes months, particularly if you have never run a marathon before. The official distance of a full marathon is 26.2 miles. In 2005, the average time to complete a marathon in the United States was 4 hours 32 minutes 8 seconds for men and 5 hours 6 minutes 8 seconds for women.

Most people who run marathons are not trying to win. Many runners try to beat their own best time. Some compare their time to other runners in the same gender and age group. Some people set time-oriented goals, such as finishing under four hours, while others try to complete the race without slowing to a walk. Many beginners simply hope to finish the marathon.

Trainers recommend that beginners maintain a consistent running schedule for six weeks prior to even starting a marathon training program. The purpose of this is to allow the body to adapt to the various physical demands of long distance running. First-time marathon runners should train by running four days a week for at least four months, increasing distance by no more than ten percent weekly. As race day approaches, runners should taper their runs, reducing the strain on their bodies and resting before the marathon. It is important not to over exert yourself during training because that can lead to lot of injuries. Most common injuries are spraining of the knees and ankles. These sprains can hinder the training.

Before the race, it is important to stretch in order to keep muscles limber. Staying hydrated is also important, but there is a danger in drinking too much water. If a runner drinks too much water, they may experience a dangerous condition called hyponatremia, a drop of sodium levels in the blood. So only drink water when you are thirsty. During the race, trainers recommend maintaining a steady pace. It is normal to feel sore after a marathon. Light exercise will help sore muscles heal faster.

Some people run marathons in pairs or groups. Training for and running a marathon with another person or group of people can make the experience more enjoyable and more rewarding. A running partner might be just the motivation you need to show up for an early morning run instead of rolling over to hit the snooze button. And, when you cross the finish line together, you can share the satisfaction of reaching your common goal.

Usually, thousands of people sign up and run a Marathon. Most people finish the race. The thrill of running a marathon for the first time is unbelievable. The training sessions are harder if you have never run before. But it is unbelievable what ones' body can do when one puts their mind to it. Having a good coach to support you makes all the difference in training for a marathon.

The daily runs are very important. Strength training and core training are also very important.

The health benefits you gain from training are tremendous. Your core muscles grow stronger, and you will have tighter thighs and gluts. Your heart will be much stronger, and you can maintain lower cholesterol and blood sugar levels. Over all, you will look better and become healthier.

Nothing can explain how people feel when they reach that finish line at the end of the race. All the hard work and months of training feel worthwhile. The feeling of accomplishing something great overtakes you. It is great to run a marathon, but it is even greater to finish it.

"Nothing can explain how people feel when they reach that finish line at the end of the race. All the hard work and months of training feel worthwhile."

10. Why are these two sentences are included in the conclusion to?

Ⓐ   leave the reader with a positive reason to run a marathon

Ⓑ   persuade the reader that anyone can run a marathon

Ⓒ   show the reader that running a marathon is not difficult

Ⓓ   change the tone of the article

Lesson 6: Author's Point of View (RI.8.6)

1.   **What is point of view?**

    Ⓐ a character's view of the action in a story

    Ⓑ the perspective from which a story is told

    Ⓒ where the author is when writing a story

    Ⓓ the view of the character in the story

2.   **Which type of point of view uses the pronouns, "I" "me" and "my"?**

    Ⓐ first person

    Ⓑ third person omniscient

    Ⓒ third person limited

    Ⓓ second person

3.   **When the narrator is one of the characters in the story, what point of view is the story being told from?**

    Ⓐ First person

    Ⓑ Third person omniscient

    Ⓒ Third person limited

    Ⓓ second person

4.   **Which of the following is true of the point of view known as third person omniscient?**

    Ⓐ The narrator is not a character in the story.

    Ⓑ The narrator is a character in the story.

    Ⓒ The narrator only knows that which he or she sees and hears.

    Ⓓ The narrator is talking about himself

5.   Which of the following is true of the point of view known as third person limited?

Ⓐ   The narrator is not a character in the story.
Ⓑ   The narrator is a character in the story.
Ⓒ   The narrator only knows that which he or she sees and hears.
Ⓓ   The narrator knows everything about all of the characters.

6.   Which type of narrator is the most reliable?

Ⓐ   first person
Ⓑ   third person limited
Ⓒ   third person omniscient
Ⓓ   second person

Marathon

Training for a marathon takes hard work and perseverance. It is not something you can do on the spur of the moment. Preparing for a marathon takes months, particularly if you have never run a marathon before. The official distance of a full marathon is 26.2 miles. In 2005, the average time to complete a marathon in the United States was 4 hours 32 minutes 8 seconds for men and 5 hours 6 minutes 8 seconds for women.

Most people who run marathons are not trying to win. Many runners try to beat their own best time. Some compare their time to other runners in the same gender and age group. Some people set time-oriented goals, such as finishing under four hours, while others try to complete the race without slowing to a walk. Many beginners simply hope to finish the marathon.

Trainers recommend that beginners maintain a consistent running schedule for six weeks prior to even starting a marathon training program. The purpose of this is to allow the body to adapt to the various physical demands of long distance running. First-time marathon runners should train by running four days a week for at least four months, increasing distance by no more than ten percent weekly. As race day approaches, runners should taper their runs, reducing the strain on their bodies and resting before the marathon. It is important not to over exert yourself during training because that can lead to lot of injuries. Most common injuries are spraining of the knees and ankles. These sprains can hinder the training.

Before the race, it is important to stretch in order to keep muscles limber. Staying hydrated is also important, but there is a danger in drinking too much water. If a runner drinks too much water, they may experience a dangerous condition called hyponatremia, a drop of sodium levels in the blood. So only drink water when you are thirsty. During the race, trainers recommend maintaining a steady pace. It is normal to feel sore after a marathon. Light exercise will help sore muscles heal faster.

Some people run marathons in pairs or groups. Training for and running a marathon with another person or group of people can make the experience more enjoyable and more rewarding. A running partner might be just the motivation you need to show up for an early morning run instead of rolling over to hit the snooze button. And, when you cross the finish line together, you can share the satisfaction of reaching your common goal.

Usually, thousands of people sign up and run a Marathon. Most people finish the race. The thrill of running a marathon for the first time is unbelievable. The training sessions are harder if you have never run before. But it is unbelievable what ones' body can do when one puts their mind to it. Having a good coach to support you makes all the difference in training for a marathon.

The daily runs are very important. Strength training and core training are also very important.

The health benefits you gain from training are tremendous. Your core muscles grow stronger, and you will have tighter thighs and gluts. Your heart will be much stronger, and you can maintain lower cholesterol and blood sugar levels. Over all, you will look better and become healthier.

Nothing can explain how people feel when they reach that finish line at the end of the race. All the hard work and months of training feel worthwhile. The feeling of accomplishing something great overtakes you. It is great to run a marathon, but it is even greater to finish it.

"Nothing can explain how people feel when they reach that finish line at the end of the race. All the hard work and months of training feel worthwhile."

"Before the race, it is important to stretch in order to keep muscles limber"

7.   What is the author's purpose in writing this sentence?

    Ⓐ   to inform
    Ⓑ   to instruct
    Ⓒ   to offer an opinion
    Ⓓ   to entertain

8.   Which point of view is the following excerpt told from?

From Chapter 1 of *Bullets and Billets* by Bruce Bainsfather

I stood in a queue of Gordons, Seaforths, Worcesters, etc., slowly moving up one, until, finally arriving at the companion (nearly said staircase), I tobogganed down into the hold, and spent what was left of the night dealing out those rations. Having finished at last, I came to the surface again, and now, as the

© Lumos Information Services 2016 | LumosLearning.com

transport glided along through the dirty waters of the river, and as I gazed at the motley collection of Frenchmen on the various wharves, and saw a variety of soldiery, and a host of other warlike "props," I felt acutely that now I was in the war at last—the real thing! For some time I had been rehearsing in England; but that was over now, and here I was—in the common or garden vernacular—"in the soup."

- Ⓐ   first person
- Ⓑ   third person omniscient
- Ⓒ   third person limited
- Ⓓ   second person

You read a research study that says eating a candy bar made of dark chocolate every day is good for your heart in the long run. The study followed the health of a large group of people over the course of ten years. You notice in fine print at the end of the research that the study was conducted by a major chocolate company.

9.   What might you, as a critical reader, take away from this?

- Ⓐ   The study must be true if it is published.
- Ⓑ   The conductors of the study benefit from the findings of this claim.
- Ⓒ   Before believing this to be true, more studies need to be done by people who don't have stakes in the particular market.
- Ⓓ   both B and C

10.   From what point of view is this story told?

It was a dark and stormy night. The people of Cape Hatteras hid indoors. Mrs. Peabody shivered, hoping the hurricane would not visit and wondering whether she would be able to fall asleep. Across the street, Mr. Greer kept watch from the high tower of his attic, certain that the hurricane would strike soon.

- Ⓐ   first person
- Ⓑ   third person limited
- Ⓒ   third person omniscient
- Ⓓ   second person

Name: _____   Date: _____

Integration of Knowledge and Ideas

Lesson 7: Publishing Mediums (RI.8.7)

1. **Which of the following is important to consider when reading a text online?**

   Ⓐ evaluate the background of the source
   Ⓑ look for why the information is being provided
   Ⓒ check the date of the source
   Ⓓ all of the above

2. **You want to write a short piece that people can respond to immediately and publicly. What is the best place to do this?**

   Ⓐ a web page
   Ⓑ the local newspaper
   Ⓒ the national newspaper
   Ⓓ a magazine

3. **You are writing an article about the stresses involved in being a high school student and what to do about them. What is the best medium of publication?**

   Ⓐ a magazine for teenagers
   Ⓑ a website aimed at teenagers
   Ⓒ a national newspaper
   Ⓓ both A and B

4. **What is the best way to learn about WWII?**

   Ⓐ to watch movies
   Ⓑ read nonfiction texts
   Ⓒ read first-hand accounts published online
   Ⓓ all of the above

© Lumos Information Services 2016 | LumosLearning.com

5. **You want to create a literary analysis of two novels. What is the best way to present this information?**

    Ⓐ in print
    Ⓑ electronically
    Ⓒ with pictures
    Ⓓ online

6. **Your teacher tells you that you must show a visual representation of a scene from a popular book. What is the best way to do this?**

    Ⓐ a movie
    Ⓑ a play
    Ⓒ an article
    Ⓓ both A and B

7. **You want to ensure you will have as few problems as possible when presenting information for your final project. What medium of publication would be best to use?**

    Ⓐ use print
    Ⓑ use electronics
    Ⓒ with pictures
    Ⓓ power point

8. **You are writing a piece on your family's history that you would like your family in the country and in Europe to read and respond to as quickly as possible. What is the best way to do this?**

    Ⓐ to write them letters and enclose the information in the letter
    Ⓑ to create a webpage for them to visit
    Ⓒ to write the history electronically and email it to them
    Ⓓ either B or C

© Lumos Information Services 2016 | LumosLearning.com

9. You want to persuade students in your school to vote for you in the upcoming student government elections. What medium of publication would be best to do this?

    Ⓐ in your school newspaper
    Ⓑ in your local newspaper
    Ⓒ on a website
    Ⓓ through a slide show

10. What is the best place to search for a specific recipe you need in a hurry?

    Ⓐ Internet
    Ⓑ magazine
    Ⓒ newspaper
    Ⓓ recipe books

© Lumos Information Services 2016 | LumosLearning.com

Lesson 8: Evaluating Author's Claims (RI.8.8)

1. **What is an author's claim?**

   - Ⓐ his or her argument
   - Ⓑ the support for his or her argument
   - Ⓒ his or her opinion
   - Ⓓ the facts for the argument

2. **What evidence must you look at in evaluating an author's claim?**

   - Ⓐ the argument itself
   - Ⓑ the support that the author provides to back up his or her argument
   - Ⓒ the author's opinion about that which he or she is arguing
   - Ⓓ how many people support the argument.

3. **What is the best way to determine the accuracy of evidence provided by the author?**

   - Ⓐ ask somebody
   - Ⓑ personal experience
   - Ⓒ look it up on the computer, any site will do
   - Ⓓ do your own research

4. **Which of the following is the least acceptable piece of evidence?**

   - Ⓐ statistics
   - Ⓑ quotes taken from a reliable source
   - Ⓒ opinion
   - Ⓓ facts

5.   Emotional appeals (appealing to the reader's emotions) should...

Ⓐ   never be used
Ⓑ   be used sometimes
Ⓒ   should always be used
Ⓓ   are never appropriate

6.   The author's evidence must...

Ⓐ   partially support the author's claims
Ⓑ   always be taken from a primary source
Ⓒ   directly support the author's claims
Ⓓ   all of the above

7.   Which of the following should you look at when examining the author's claim?

Ⓐ   What is the author's purpose?
Ⓑ   What are the sources that the author has cited?
Ⓒ   Does the author's evidence several times to make sure it sound strong?
Ⓓ   What is the purpose of the evidence?

The Necessity of Exercise

(1) 58 million Americans are overweight (getfitamerica.com). (2) This number is and has been on a steady rise. More and more Americans are exercising less and less. (3) The Center for Disease Control recommends 2.5 hours of moderate aerobic activity each week, along with 2 days of strength training. (4) Americans are clearly not abiding by these minimum recommendations, as the numbers prove. (5) It is necessary for Americans to get more exercise in order to lead healthy lives. (6) There is no good reason for healthy people not to exercise, but the there are many benefits, including maintaining a healthy weight, relieving everyday stress and lowering one's chances for certain diseases.

8.   Which of the sentences above includes the author's argument?

Ⓐ   3
Ⓑ   4
Ⓒ   5
Ⓓ   6

© Lumos Information Services 2016 | LumosLearning.com

9.   **According to the author's introduction, what points do you expect that he or she will be providing evidence for?**

   (A)   how much exercise people need
   (B)   how much exercise one needs to maintain a healthy weight
   (C)   how exercise raises everyday stress
   (D)   how exercise increases risk for certain diseases

10.   **Which of the author's statements provides evidence?**

   (A)   1
   (B)   2
   (C)   3
   (D)   4
   (E)   5

© Lumos Information Services 2016 | LumosLearning.com

Lesson 9: Conflicting Information (RI.8.9)

1. **When you come across two conflicting viewpoints, what should you do?**

    Ⓐ research other sources to find out which fact is correct
    Ⓑ look to see if the fact may have changed
    Ⓒ examine the reliability of both writers
    Ⓓ all of the above

2. **Determine whether the writers are presenting conflicting information based on fact or interpretation.**

    Writer One: Geology is a branch of science.
    Writer Two: Geology is a branch of math.

    Ⓐ fact
    Ⓑ opinion

3. **Determine whether the writers are presenting conflicting information based on fact or interpretation.**

    Writer One: The president's sweater was too small.
    Writer Two: The president's sweater fit him well.

    Ⓐ fact
    Ⓑ opinion

4. **Determine whether the writers are presenting conflicting information based on fact or interpretation.**

    Writer One: The worst storm of the season passed through Seattle yesterday.
    Writer Two: A moderate storm passed through Seattle yesterday.

    Ⓐ fact
    Ⓑ opinion

© Lumos Information Services 2016 | LumosLearning.com

5. **Which of the following is an example of a fact that could change?**

    (A) someone's name
    (B) the location of a store
    (C) the area of a park
    (C) all of the above

6. **Determine whether the conflicting information presented by the two authors is fact or interpretation.**

    Einstein

    Albert Einstein was born on March 14th, 1879, in the German city of Ulm, without any indication that he was destined for greatness.

    Einstein

    Albert Einstein was born March 15, 1879, in the city of Ulm. When he was born, people did not think he was going to be anything special.

    (A) fact
    (B) interpretation

7. **Determine whether the following is fact or opinion.**

    Bailey is wearing blue shoes.

    (A) fact
    (B) opinion

8. **Determine whether the following is fact or opinion.**

    Dr. Blair studied at the most prestigious of schools, Harvard University.

    (A) fact
    (B) opinion
    (C) both

© Lumos Information Services 2016 | LumosLearning.com

9. **Which of the following is not a reason for the differing interpretations between texts?**

   Ⓐ The authors are trying to prove different points.
   Ⓑ One or both of the authors may be trying to persuade the reader to believe one way.
   Ⓒ The authors are both trying to be objective.
   Ⓓ Subjectivity is often apparent in writing.

10. **Determine whether the following is fact or opinion.**

The atrocious painting sold for $1,000,000.

   Ⓐ fact
   Ⓑ opinion
   Ⓒ both

End of Reading: Informational Text

© Lumos Information Services 2016 | LumosLearning.com

Reading: Informational Text

Answer Key
&
Detailed Explanations

© Lumos Information Services 2016 | LumosLearning.com

Lesson 1: Making Inferences Based on Textual Evidence (RI.8.1)

Question	Answer	Detailed Explanation
1.	B	Answer choice B is correct. It is the definition of inference.
2.	C	Answer choice C is correct. The proper way to cite evidence from a text is to put it in quotes.
3.	D	Answer D is the correct choice. All three methods are acceptable ways of citing evidence.
4.	A	Answer choice A is correct because it asked about the discovery, not actually trying to create. Answers B and C both have to do with experimenting, not discovering.
5.	B	Answer choice B is correct because it talks about the success of the experiment. Answer choice A is about the discovery of the idea, and answer choice C is about the trial and error of the experiment.
6.	C	Answer choice C is correct because it talks about how they tried "many more experiments".
7.	C	Answer choice C is correct because it says the parents take turns, which leads readers to believe they are sharing responsibility.
8.	D	Answer D is correct. There is nothing in the text that suggests what the penguins do for survival after the chick is born.
9.	A	Answer choice A is the correct answer because the text states that, "He seemed always to be laughing..." and continued to discuss how he engaged happily with the children. Answers B and C are incorrect because there is no evidence to support those conclusions.
10.	C	Answer C is correct because the text implies that the author met the captain before the civil war began.

© Lumos Information Services 2016 | LumosLearning.com

Lesson 2: Central Ideas (RI.8.2)

Question	Answer	Detailed Explanation
1.	D	Answer choice D is correct. The central idea is the main idea in a piece of informational text. Answer choice A is incorrect because the central idea may not be easily located in the topic sentence. Answer choice B is incorrect because a central idea is located in informational text rather than literature which is generally fiction. Answer choice C is incorrect because an informational piece may not be about a person.
2.	D	Answer choice D is correct. Central idea is found in nonfiction and all of the pieces are nonfiction.
3.	D	Answer choice D is correct. The central idea is supported by details in the text; It can sometimes be found in the title of the text, and covers the whole text.
4.	D	Answer choice D is correct. When determining the main idea, it is important not to confuse the main idea with the topic (what the passage is about) and the supporting details. The supporting details work to support the main idea.
5.	B	Answer choice B is correct. The Montgolfier brothers theorized that hot air would make a balloon rise and conducted an experiment to prove their theory. Answer choice A is incorrect because the central idea is what the brothers did. It is not about why they were famous. Answer choice C is incorrect because there is nothing in the passage about the brothers losing their jobs.
6.	C	Answer choice C is correct. Emperor penguins lay their eggs in the Antarctic and take turns caring for the egg until it hatches. Answer choice A is incorrect because it is not the central idea of the text. Answer choice B is incorrect because the central idea includes both the location and caring of the egg.
7.	B	Answer choice B is correct. The central idea of this piece of informational text is the study of archaeology. Answer choice A is incorrect because the central idea is not the origin of archaeology as the origins are uncertain. Answer choice C is incorrect because the text is not at all about anthropology. Answer choice D is incorrect because the text is not only about the study of the human past.
8.	A	Answer choice A is correct. Archaeologists study past human life and culture by examining the things left behind by early humans. Answer choice B is incorrect because archaeologists study humans and their culture. Answer choice C is incorrect because archaeologists study not only humans and possibly their families, but also their culture.
9.	A	Answer choice A is correct. The passage is mainly about the health benefits of quinoa.
10.	B	Answer choice B is correct. The central idea of the passage is about how to cook quinoa. All the details support this central idea.

© Lumos Information Services 2016 | LumosLearning.com

Lesson 3: Connections and Distinctions (RI.8.3)

Question	Answer	Detailed Explanation
1.	B	Answer B is correct. To find distinctions is to find differences.
2.	A	Answer choice A is correct. A connection is a similarity between the reader and something he understands.
3.	D	Answer choice D is correct. They both focus on all of the above.
4.	B	Answer choice B is correct. While it can be studied in all the places, a museum is the best place to see the many different examples of it.
5.	A	Answer choice A is correct because the text points out one distinction between the types of quinoa.
6.	D	Answer D is correct. They are all ways that marathons are different than other competitions.
7.	A	Answer A is correct. The article mentions in the beginning that it's not competitive; therefore, answers B and C are incorrect.
8.	B	Answer B is correct. The similarity between this ad and many other ads is the small print.
9.	C	Answer C is correct. The idiom "in the soup" means in a bad situation.
10.	A	Answer A is the correct answer because the narrator says he has arrived at the war.

© Lumos Information Services 2016 | LumosLearning.com

Lesson 4: Determining Meaning of Words (RI.8.4)

Question	Answer	Detailed Explanation
1.	B	Answer choice B is correct. A connotation is the meaning of the word with regard to its use in context.
2.	A	Detonation means the actual meaning of a wordd. In other words, it is the dictionary definition of the word. Hence, answer choice A is correct.
3.	C	Answer choice C is correct. To trek means to walk a long distance.
4.	A	Answer choice A is correct. The way a field turns into a profession is professionalization.
5.	A	Answer choice A is correct. When one does something systematically, he follows a very specific procedure.
6.	C	Answer choice C is correct. To overexert means to do more than your body can handle.
7.	A	Answer choice A is correct. In the spur of moment means taking immediate decisions without thinking. In this context also it means that training for Marathon requires determination, hard work and commitment and it cannot be something that can be done instantaneously.
8.	B	Answer choice B is correct. The phrase is meant to set up a serious tone so readers understand the complexity of running a marathon.
9.	A	Answer choice A is correct. Readers can assume they are ranks in the military because the narrator is on a military ship traveling to a battle.
10.	A	Answer choice A is the correct answer. The various references to the theater imply that he is comparing a theater to war. Hence, it is an implied metaphor.

© Lumos Information Services 2016 | LumosLearning.com

Lesson 5: Analyzing Structures in Text (RI 8.5)

Question	Answer	Detailed Explanation
1.	D	Answer choice D is correct. When trying to determine the structure of a piece of text, it is important to look at the genre of writing, the author's purpose and the types of transition words use.
2.	B	Answer choice B is correct. Unlike nonfiction, a fictional story will have a plot.
3.	B	Answer choice B is correct. Words such as "unlike", "as well as", "on the other hand", and "in contrast", are all indicative of a comparison.
4.	A	Answer choice A is correct. Adding an introductory and concluding paragraph would turn this passage into an essay. Remember an essay must have an introduction, body, and conclusion.
5.	A	Answer choice A is correct. The key words are first, soon afterwards, after this, and eventually. These words indicate a sequence of event.
6.	C	Answer choice C is correct. The passage was written to describe the egg laying routine of the Emperor Penguin. There are no clue words to lead the reader to believe there is any sequencing, comparing/contrasting, or cause/effect included in the passage.
7.	D	Answer choice D is correct. The author uses this introductory sentence to give the reader some background information on archaeology and what the article is about.
8.	A	Answer choice A is correct. This sentence is included to inform the reader why archaeology is important. It is important to note that authors have a reason for every piece of text they include in any piece of writing.
9.	D	Answer choice D is correct. This sentence is included so that readers will understand that archaeology has been happening for a very long time.
10.	A	Answer choice A is correct. These two sentences have a positive connotation in an effort to leave the reader with a positive opinion about running.

© Lumos Information Services 2016 | LumosLearning.com

Lesson 6: Author's Point of View (RI.8.6)

Question	Answer	Detailed Explanation
1.	B	Answer choice B is correct. Point of view is the perspective from which the story or text is written.
2.	A	Answer choice A is correct. First person point of view is written from the narrator's point of view and will include personal pronouns.
3.	A	Answer choice A is correct. When the narrator is in the story, in other words, he or she is telling the story, the story is being told from the first person point of view.
4.	A	Answer choice A is correct. A third person omniscient narrator is not included as a character in the story. The third person omniscient narrator knows the thoughts and feelings of all the characters in the story.
5.	A	Answer choice A is correct. A third person limited narrator is not a character in the story. The third person limited narrator only knows the thoughts and feelings of one character. This is unlike the third person omniscient narrator who knows the thoughts and feelings of all the characters.
6.	C	Answer choice C is correct. The most reliable narrator is the third person omniscient narrator because he or she knows the thoughts and feelings of all the characters.
7.	B	Answer choice B is correct. This line was written to instruct those unfamiliar with running on what they should do prior to a run.
8.	A	Answer choice A is correct. This excerpt is written in first person point of view. Note the use of the personal pronoun "I."
9.	D	Answer choice D is correct. If the research was done by a company with ties to chocolate, chances are the data was collected or interpreted in a way to make it appear that eating chocolate is beneficial. It is best to rely on research conducted by independent research facilities.
10.	C	Answer choice C is correct. The narrator knows the thoughts and feelings of both characters in the story.

Lesson 7: Publishing Mediums (RI.8.7)

Question	Answer	Detailed Explanation
1.	D	Answer choice D is correct. When reading text online, it is important to evaluate the source of the information, author's purpose, and date of the source.
2.	A	Answer choice A is correct. The fastest place to publish and get public responses is on a webpage on the internet.
3.	D	Answer choice D is correct. The best place, and likeliest to reach the most readers, is via a teen magazine AND a website targeting teen audiences.
4.	D	Answer choice D is correct. Remember, though, that movies will take liberties with facts. Primary sources will give accurate information, but you should incorporate nonfiction text in with your research, as well. Using as many data sources as possible in research will allow for a more thorough paper.
5.	A	Answer choice A is correct. The best way to present a literary analysis is in print, like an essay.
6.	D	Answer choice D is correct. The best way to show a visual representation of a book is via a short movie you film yourself or a play you create yourself.
7.	A	Answer choice A is correct. Using electronics when presenting means always having to depend on something electronic to work. A paper presentation never fails to load or suffer from an unavoidable systems crash.
8.	D	Answer choice D is correct. Creating something online would be the fastest way to disseminate the information. Writing a letter and mailing it would be more personal, but if time is of the essence, then using the electronic route is by far less time consuming.
9.	A	Answer choice A is correct. The best place to campaign for a school office is in the school newspaper.
10.	A	Answer choice A is correct. If you need a specific recipe in a hurry, the fastest place to get the information is by doing a web search on the Internet. You can use specific terms which should then navigate you to the appropriate sites.

© Lumos Information Services 2016 | LumosLearning.com

Lesson 8: Evaluating Authors Claims (RI.8.8)

Question	Answer	Detailed Explanation
1.	A	Answer choice A is correct. An author's claim is something an author is trying to convince you of that hasn't been proven. Once proven, it becomes a fact.
2.	B	Answer choice B is correct. When evaluating an author's claim, you must be a careful reader of the support he or she provides for the claim.
3.	D	Answer choice D is correct. If you are in doubt of an author's claim, do some research on your own. Look up information on the internet using sites that are dependable or use other research tools such as books and encyclopedias.
4.	C	Answer choice C is correct. An author who bases his or her claim primarily on opinion does not provide acceptable proof. Opinions are the least acceptable tools to use when making a claim.
5.	B	Answer choice B is correct. Emotional appeals should be used sparingly because, while they can be effective, they tend to be weak.
6.	C	Answer choice C is correct. Evidence used to support an author's claim should always be supportive of the claim.
7.	A	Answer choice A is correct. When examining an author's claim, you should always try to determine his/her purpose. Is the author trying to sell you something or simply provide information? Be a careful reader.
8.	D	Answer choice D is correct. The author's claim is at the end of the paragraph.
9.	B	Answer choice B is correct. Based on the introduction, sentence one and two, the reader should expect to read about how much exercise is needed to maintain a healthy weight.
10.	A	Answer choice A is correct. This is statistical evidence. As a careful reader, you should consider navigating to the website mentioned to verify this statistic. Additionally, a careful reader will check the sources used to gather this data.

© Lumos Information Services 2016 | LumosLearning.com

Lesson 9: Conflicting Information (RI.8.9)

Question	Answer	Detailed Explanation
1.	D	Answer choice D is correct. When faced with conflicting information, it is a good idea to do further research. Remember, facts can sometimes change. For example, advances in medicine can change what we believe are facts about health. Additionally, checking the credibility of the authors is a good idea.
2.	A	Answer choice A is correct. Geology is a science and this can be verified or proven.
3.	B	Answer choice B is correct. Whether or not the president's sweater is too small is an opinion. Some people may prefer a snugger fit than others. The conflicting information is based on opinion.
4.	B	Answer choice B is correct. The ferocity of a storm is an opinion; therefore, the conflicting interpretation is opinion.
5.	D	Answer choice D is correct. All three choices could be proven, but could also change. When a woman gets married, she may choose to take her husband's last name; thus, her name changes. If a store chooses not to renew its lease and moves to a cheaper location, it's former location, which could be proven, is no longer valid. The same goes for a park. If a park's original location isn't large enough to accommodate an extension, its location may be moved.
6.	A	Answer choice A is correct. Birthdates are verifiable; therefore, the conflicting information is based on fact. Additionally, the statements of what Einestein might be is documented fact.
7.	A	Answer choice A is correct. The color of Bailey's shoes can be proven.
8.	C	Answer choice C is correct. There is both a fact and an opinion in the statement. Dr. Blair's university training can be verified, therefore, it is a fact. Whether or not Harvard is the most prestigious university is an opinion. Be careful you do not let a sentence with mixed information misguide you. Even in nonfiction, authors have bias.
9.	C	Answer choice C is correct. When authors write, they have a purpose in mind. Many times their interpretation of data is skewed to fit the intentions of the author.
10.	C	Answer choice C is correct. Evidently the person who purchased the painting for $1,000,000 (which is verifiable) did not believe the painting to be atrocious. Therefore, the statement included both a fact and an opinion.

© Lumos Information Services 2016 | LumosLearning.com

Language

Conventions of Standard English

Lesson 1: Adjectives and Adverbs (L.8.1.A)

1. **What is an adjective?**

    Ⓐ a word that modifies (describes) a verb
    Ⓑ a word that modifies (describes) a noun in a sentence
    Ⓒ a word that modifies (describes) a sentence
    Ⓓ a word that modifies (describes) descriptive words

2. **What is an adverb?**

    Ⓐ a word that modifies (describes) adjectives
    Ⓑ a word that modifies (describes) verbs
    Ⓒ a word that modifies (describes) adverbs
    Ⓓ a word that modifies (describes) descriptive words

3. **A lot of people have trouble with the words "good" and "well". See if you can use them correctly in the following sentences by choosing the correct the words in correct sequence.**

    a) I am _____.

    b) Dinner was really _____.

    c) They are _____ baseball players.

    d) You play really _____.

    Ⓐ well, well, good, good
    Ⓑ well, good, well, good
    Ⓒ well, good, good, good
    Ⓓ well, good, good, well

© Lumos Information Services 2016 | LumosLearning.com

4.   Choose the correct adjective/ adverb sequence for the following sentences.

a) I stayed home from school because when I woke up this morning I felt (bad/ badly).

b) I did (good/ well) on my science test.

c) I answered the question as (honest/ honestly) as I could.

- Ⓐ   bad, good, honest
- Ⓑ   badly, well, honestly
- Ⓒ   bad, well, honestly
- Ⓓ   badly, well, honestly

5.   Which choice is the adverb that correctly completes the following sentence?

I am very fond of Miss Jenkins; she teaches very _____.

- Ⓐ   patiently
- Ⓑ   patient
- Ⓒ   patience
- Ⓓ   patiented

6.   Which word is the adverb in the following sentence?

She picked up the sweet baby very carefully.

- Ⓐ   sweet
- Ⓑ   very
- Ⓒ   carefully
- Ⓓ   both B and C

7.   Which word in the following sentence is an adjective?

After a long afternoon at practice, I am tired, hungry, and dirty.

- Ⓐ   tired
- Ⓑ   hungry
- Ⓒ   dirty
- Ⓓ   all of the above

© Lumos Information Services 2016 | LumosLearning.com

8.   **What is the adjective in the following sentence?**

The pretty girl brushed her hair before she went to bed.

   Ⓐ   pretty
   Ⓑ   girl
   Ⓒ   brushed
   Ⓓ   hair

9.   **What is the adverb in the following sentence?**

He slowly walked towards the elevator on his floor.

   Ⓐ   slowly
   Ⓑ   elevator
   Ⓒ   floor
   Ⓓ   walked

10.   **What is the adverb in the following sentence?**

Jimmy sadly walked away after having lost a tough game of baseball.

   Ⓐ   sadly
   Ⓑ   lost
   Ⓒ   tough
   Ⓓ   baseball

© Lumos Information Services 2016 | LumosLearning.com

Lesson 2: Subject-Verb Agreement (L.8.1.B)

1.   Select the correct verb form to agree with the subject in the following sentence.

Either the teacher or the principal _____ going to contact you.

- Ⓐ are
- Ⓑ is
- Ⓒ not
- Ⓓ never

2.   Which sentence shows the correct subject-verb agreement?

a) Neither the cat nor the dogs have been fed.

b) Neither the cat nor the dogs has been fed.

- Ⓐ a
- Ⓑ b

3.   Select the correct verb form to agree with the subject in the following sentence.

_____ my sister or my parents going to pick me up?

- Ⓐ Is
- Ⓑ Are
- Ⓒ you're
- Ⓓ watching

4.   Select the correct verb form to agree with the subject in the following sentence.

Some of the answers _____ to have been wrong.

- Ⓐ seems
- Ⓑ seem
- Ⓒ just
- Ⓓ really

© Lumos Information Services 2016 | LumosLearning.com

5.   Select the correct verb form to agree with the subject in the following sentence.

Mary and Joe _____ going to the dance together.

- Ⓐ   is
- Ⓑ   are
- Ⓒ   wouldn't
- Ⓓ   walking

6.   Select the correct verb form to agree with the subject in the following sentence.

The highlighter or the marker _____ in the side drawer.

- Ⓐ   is
- Ⓑ   are
- Ⓒ   rolling
- Ⓓ   writing

7.   Select the correct verb form to agree with the subject in the following sentence.

The student, along with his parents, _____ coming to the talent show.

- Ⓐ   is
- Ⓑ   are
- Ⓒ   never
- Ⓓ   walking

8.   Select the correct verb form to agree with the subject in the following sentence.

Neither the tomatoes nor the mint in my garden have begun to grow.

- Ⓐ   the subject closest to the verb
- Ⓑ   the subject farthest from the verb
- Ⓒ   it doesn't matter which subject is used

© Lumos Information Services 2016 | LumosLearning.com

9.   Identify the subject(s) in the following sentence.

Some of the food is spoiled because it was sitting in the sun too long.

- Ⓐ   some
- Ⓑ   food
- Ⓒ   some and food
- Ⓓ   sun

10.   Identify the subject(s) in the following sentence.

Either the teacher or the principal is going to contact you regarding your grades.

- Ⓐ   teacher
- Ⓑ   principal
- Ⓒ   teacher and principal
- Ⓓ   grades

© Lumos Information Services 2016 | LumosLearning.com

Lesson 3: Pronouns (L.8.1.C)

1. **Select the pronoun that will best fit into the following sentence.**

The instructor put _____ students at ease when he said no one would fail.

- Ⓐ we
- Ⓑ his
- Ⓒ their
- Ⓓ them

2. **Select the pronoun that will best fit into the following sentence.**

My grandmother and _____ enjoyed spending the day together at the fair.

- Ⓐ I
- Ⓑ myself
- Ⓒ me
- Ⓓ my

3. **Select the pronoun that will best fit into the following sentence.**

_____ students laughed so loudly that the class next door was distracted from their lesson.

- Ⓐ We
- Ⓑ Us
- Ⓒ Them
- Ⓓ Those

4. **To what does the demonstrative pronoun "that" refer to in the following sentences?**

I saw a terrible skateboarding accident down the street. That was awful.

- Ⓐ the skateboarding accident
- Ⓑ being in the street
- Ⓒ seeing the skateboard down the street
- Ⓓ the awful thing

© Lumos Information Services 2016 | LumosLearning.com

5.   Choose the correct pronoun in the sentence below.

The woman (who/whom) is wearing the red dress would like to make a reservation.

Ⓐ   who
Ⓑ   whom

6.   Choose the correct pronoun in the sentence below.

With (who/whom) were you speaking?

Ⓐ   who
Ⓑ   whom

7.   Choose the correct pronoun in the sentence below.

(Who/whom) can you send to help us?

Ⓐ   who
Ⓑ   whom

8.   Identify the pronoun in the following sentence.

Martha's sister wanted her siblings to give her something exciting for her birthday.

Ⓐ   Martha
Ⓑ   sister
Ⓒ   birthday
Ⓓ   her

9.   To what does the demonstrative pronoun "those" refer to in the following sentences?

Since I was going to be carting furniture up and down stairs, I put on my favorite pair of shoes. My daughter looked me over once and said, "You're wearing those?"

Ⓐ   the shirt
Ⓑ   the shoes
Ⓒ   the shorts
Ⓓ   the whole look

10. Identify the pronoun in the following sentence.

Mike's mother told him that the trash needed to be taken out sooner rather than later.

- Ⓐ Mike
- Ⓑ mother
- Ⓒ him
- Ⓓ trash

Lesson 4: Phrases and Clauses (L.8.1.C)

1. **Which of the following sentences is an infinitive phrase?**

    Ⓐ To make my birthday special, my family threw me a surprise party.
    Ⓑ My teacher, the one wearing the blue dress, gave us our final yesterday.
    Ⓒ Mary waited at the bus stop, hoping another would come by.
    Ⓓ On the side of the road, we saw a perfectly good couch.

2. **Identify whether the following is an independent or subordinate clause.**

    The boy cried.

    Ⓐ independent
    Ⓑ subordinate

3. **Identify whether the following is an independent or subordinate clause.**

    When I jumped down

    Ⓐ independent
    Ⓑ subordinate

4. **Identify whether the following is an independent or subordinate clause.**

    He stopped.

    Ⓐ independent
    Ⓑ subordinate

5. **Identify whether the following is an independent or subordinate clause:**

    If he had run

    Ⓐ independent
    Ⓑ subordinate

© Lumos Information Services 2016 | LumosLearning.com

6.   What is an independent clause?

Ⓐ It has a subject and verb and can be a complete sentence by itself.
Ⓑ It has a subject and a verb but cannot stand by itself as a complete sentence.
Ⓒ It is only part of a sentence.
Ⓓ It does not have either a subject or a verb and is therefore not a sentence.

7.   What is a subordinate clause?

Ⓐ It has a subject and verb and can be a complete sentence by itself.
Ⓑ It has a subject and a verb but cannot stand by itself as a complete sentence.
Ⓒ It is only two words.
Ⓓ It does not have either a subject or a verb and is therefore not a sentence.

8.   What is an adjective phrase?

Ⓐ It modifies a noun.
Ⓑ It modifies a verb, adverb, or adjective.
Ⓒ It tells "what kind" or "which one".
Ⓓ both A and C

9.   What does the following sentence contain?

The dog with the bright blue collar jumped on me.

Ⓐ an adverb phrase
Ⓑ an adjective phrase

10.   What type of phrase does the following sentence have?

Because she did not clean her room, Bethany lost her iPad privileges for the weekend.

Ⓐ adjective
Ⓑ adverb
Ⓒ gerund
Ⓓ noun

© Lumos Information Services 2016 | LumosLearning.com

Lesson 5: Verbals (L.8.1.D)

1. **What is the definition of a verbal?**

    Ⓐ a spoken form of communication
    Ⓑ forms of verbs that function as other parts of speech
    Ⓒ a very descriptive word
    Ⓓ a word that contains a sound

2. **Which verbals function as adjectives?**

    Ⓐ infinitives
    Ⓑ participles
    Ⓒ gerunds
    Ⓓ nounes

3. **Which verbals function as nouns?**

    Ⓐ infinitives
    Ⓑ gerunds
    Ⓒ participles
    Ⓓ verbs

4. **Which verbals function as nouns, adjectives, or adverbials?**

    Ⓐ gerunds
    Ⓑ infinitives
    Ⓒ participles
    Ⓓ verbs

© Lumos Information Services 2016 | LumosLearning.com

5. **Which of the following sentences uses the verbal known as an infinitive?**

    Ⓐ Looking back through the photo albums gives me fond memories of the time I spent in Italy with my grandparents.

    Ⓑ My cousins like to visit the beach when they come to our house, since they live in the mountains.

    Ⓒ She was terminated from her job because she was never on time.

    Ⓓ Kelsey recieved the best present for her birthday

6. **Which of the following sentences uses the verbal known as a gerund?**

    Ⓐ Sarah enjoys hiking on the local trails.

    Ⓑ My older sister is going to go off to college at the end of summer.

    Ⓒ I really enjoy giving special gifts to my friends and family members on their birthdays.

    Ⓓ My favorite time of the year is summar vacation.

7. **Which of the following sentences uses the verbal known as a participle.**

    Ⓐ After school, my friends and I are going to go to the mall.

    Ⓑ The soup boiling on the stove smells delicious.

    Ⓒ I walked my dog around the block.

    Ⓓ My friends are coming over after school today.

8. **What part of speech is the verbal taking in the following sentence?**

    The sparkling ring is beautiful.

    Ⓐ noun
    Ⓑ adjective
    Ⓒ verb
    Ⓓ adverb

9.   What part of speech is the verbal taking in the following sentence?

The bird was sleeping in its nest.

- Ⓐ   noun
- Ⓑ   adjective
- Ⓒ   verb
- Ⓓ   adverb

10.   What part of speech is the verbal taking in the following sentence?

The sound of running water became louder and louder.

- Ⓐ   noun
- Ⓑ   adjective
- Ⓒ   verb
- Ⓓ   adverb

© Lumos Information Services 2016 | LumosLearning.com

Lesson 6: Active and Passive Voice (L.8.3.A)

1. **What comes first in active voice?**

    Ⓐ subject
    Ⓑ object
    Ⓒ action
    Ⓓ fall

2. **What is passive voice?**

    Ⓐ when the writer uses a very nice tone of voice
    Ⓑ when the writer says nice things
    Ⓒ a sentence that is not a question or command
    Ⓓ a sentence in which the subject is acted upon instead of doing the action

3. **What is active voice?**

    Ⓐ when somebody talks a lot
    Ⓑ a sentence with a lot of action
    Ⓒ a sentence in which the subject is performing the action
    Ⓓ when someone talks and performs an activity at the same time

4. **Is the following sentence written in active or passive voice?**

    Margaret is loved by Brian.

    Ⓐ active
    Ⓑ passive
    Ⓒ neither
    Ⓓ both

5. **Is the following sentence written in active or passive voice?**

The stray dog was being taking care of by Matthew.

- (A) active
- (B) passive
- (C) neither
- (D) both

6. **Is the following sentence written in active or passive voice?**

Samantha sewed the hem of her sister's wedding dress when it ripped.

- (A) active
- (B) passive
- (C) neither
- (D) both

7. **Which of the following sentences is written in active voice?**

a) One day that dress will be handed down to me by my mother.

b) My father always changes the oil in our vehicles by himself.

c) I made chocolate chip cookies for the birthday party.

d) That cabinet was made by my grandfather.

- (A) a and b
- (B) b and c
- (C) d and c
- (D) a and d

© Lumos Information Services 2016 | LumosLearning.com

8. **Which of the following sentences are written in active voice?**

a) This house was built by my uncle.

b) This wonderful dessert was baked by my mother.

Ⓐ a

Ⓑ b

Ⓒ both a and b

Ⓓ none of the above

9. **Which of the following sentences is written in active voice?**

a) Everybody should eat vegetables.

b) At the concert, one audience member will be selected to participate.

c) Everyone should learn how to swim as early as possible.

Ⓐ a

Ⓑ b

Ⓒ c

Ⓓ all of the above

Ⓔ none of the above

10. **Which of the following sentences is written in passive voice.**

a) One day, that dress will be handed down to me by my mother.

b) My father always changes the oil in our vehicles by himself.

c) I made chocolate chip cookies for the birthday party.

d) My grandfather made that cabinet.

Ⓐ a

Ⓑ b

Ⓒ c

Ⓓ d

Lesson 7: Punctuation (L.8.2.A)

1. **Determine which sentence shows the correct usage of the comma.**

    Ⓐ Please pick up glue, scissors, and construction paper.
    Ⓑ The names of my pets are, Max, Goldie, and Emily.
    Ⓒ I looked everywhere for my keys, including the trash and under the couch and in the kitchen.
    Ⓓ My father Jim and my mother Martha enjoy camping dancing and jogging together.

2. **The following sentence is missing one or more commas. Determine which example shows the correct comma placement.**

    Ⓐ My uncle, who is an incredibly talented actor encouraged me to try out in the talent show.
    Ⓑ My uncle who is an incredibly talented actor, encouraged me to try out in the talent show.
    Ⓒ My uncle, who is an incredibly talented actor, encouraged me to try out for the talent show.
    Ⓓ My uncle who, is an incredibly talented actor, encouraged me to try out for the talent show.

3. **How would you fix the following sentence?**

    After you have finished taking out the trash you may watch your favorite show.

    Ⓐ After you have finished, taking out the trash you may watch your favorite show.
    Ⓑ After you have finished taking out the trash, you may watch your favorite show.
    Ⓒ After, you have finished taking out the trash you may watch your favorite show.
    Ⓓ After you have finished taking out the trash you may watch your favorite show.

4. **Select the sentence that shows the correct usage of the semicolon.**

    Ⓐ Her uncle is coming to visit; and he is traveling from far away.
    Ⓑ This summer we went camping; always fun.
    Ⓒ I enjoy the arts; I especially love to paint with watercolors.
    Ⓓ I enjoy the arts and; I especially love to paint with watercolors.

© Lumos Information Services 2016 | LumosLearning.com

5. **Determine which sentence shows the correct usage of the apostrophe.**

   (A) That girl is Mrs. Jones's daughter.
   (B) That girl is Mrs. Jones' daughter.
   (C) That girl is Mrs. Jones daughter.
   (D) That girl is Mrs'. Jones' daughter.

6. **Which of the following is the plural possessive form of "mice"?**

   (A) mices
   (B) mices'
   (C) mice's
   (D) mouse's

7. **Determine which sentence shows the correct usage of the apostrophe and comma.**

   (A) I couldn't wait to see Katie's new dog, Alfie.
   (B) I couldn't wait to see Katies new dog, Alfie.
   (C) I couldn't wait to see Katie new dog Alfie.
   (D) I couldn't wait to see Katie's new dog Alfie.

8. **Which of the following does the contraction "would've" take the place of?**

   (A) would of
   (B) would have
   (C) will of
   (D) will have

© Lumos Information Services 2016 | LumosLearning.com

9.   What is the best way to fix the following sentence?

Yvettes invitation for Brendas surprise party said to bring the following things to the party cupcakes soda and a gag gift

- Ⓐ   Yvette's invitation for Brendas surprise party said to bring the following things to the party: cupcakes, soda and a gag gift.
- Ⓑ   Yvette's invitation for Brenda's surprise party said to bring the following things to the party: cupcakes, soda, and a gag gift.
- Ⓒ   Yvettes invitation for Brenda's surprise party said to bring the following things to the party: cupcakes, soda, and a gag gift.
- Ⓓ   Yvette's invitation for Brenda's surprise party said to bring the following things to the party; cupcakes, soda and a gag gift.

10.   Where would you include a dash in the following sentence?

Kasey had not taken the time to read the directions no wonder the bookcase fell apart after an hour!

- Ⓐ   Kasey had not taken the time to read the directions, no wonder the bookcase - fell apart after an hour!
- Ⓑ   Kasey - had not taken the time to read the directions, no wonder the bookcase fell apart after an hour!
- Ⓒ   Kasey had not taken the time to read the directions - no wonder the bookcase fell apart after an hour!
- Ⓓ   Kasey had not taken the time to read - the directions- no wonder the bookcase fell apart after an hour!

© Lumos Information Services 2016 | LumosLearning.com

Lesson 8: Ellipsis (L.8.2.B)

1. **Which of the following symbols is an ellipsis?**

   Ⓐ ...
   Ⓑ ;
   Ⓒ :
   Ⓓ –

2. **What is the purpose of an ellipsis?**

   Ⓐ to indicate text has been omitted
   Ⓑ to make the reader think about a point
   Ⓒ to end sentence powerfully
   Ⓓ to emphasize a specific fact

3. **An ellipsis can be used to create suspense.**

   Ⓐ True
   Ⓑ False

4. **You cannot use an ellipsis at the beginning of a sentence.**

   Ⓐ True
   Ⓑ False

5. **If an ellipsis comes at the end of the sentence, add it after the period for a total of 4 dots, so it looks like this....**

   Ⓐ True
   Ⓑ False

6. **The following is the correct use of an ellipsis.**

   "I don't know...I'm not sure...What do you think?"

   Ⓐ True
   Ⓑ False

© Lumos Information Services 2016 | LumosLearning.com

7.   When is it appropriate to use an ellipsis?

Ⓐ   when citing evidence from a text that is long
Ⓑ   when researching and information is at the beginning and end of a paragraph
Ⓒ   when trying to be concise and only use necessary facts
Ⓓ   all of the above

8.   What is the appropriate way to cite the following information?

58 million Americans are overweight (getfitamerica.com). This number is and has been on a steady rise. More and more Americans are exercising less and less. The Center for Disease Control recommends 2.5 hours of moderate aerobic activity each week, along with 2 days of strength training. Americans are clearly not abiding by these minimum recommendations, as the numbers prove. It is necessary for Americans to get more exercise in order to lead a healthy life. There is no good reason for healthy people not to exercise but the there are many benefits including maintaining a healthy weight, relieving everyday stress and lowering one's chances for certain diseases.

Ⓐ   After examining the facts, it is evident that Americans need exercise. A recent article explained, "58 million Americans are overweight– It is necessary for Americans to get more exercise in order to lead a healthy life."

Ⓑ   After examining the facts, it is evident that Americans need exercise. A recent article explained, "58 million Americans are overweight: It is necessary for Americans to get more exercise in order to lead a healthy life."

Ⓒ   After examining the facts, it is evident that Americans need exercise. A recent article explained, "58 million Americans are overweight... It is necessary for Americans to get more exercise in order to lead a healthy life."

Ⓓ   none of the above

9.   The following sentence properly uses an ellipsis?

"...[T]here are many benefits including maintaining a healthy weight, relieving everyday stress and lowering one's chances for certain diseases."

Ⓐ   True
Ⓑ   False

© Lumos Information Services 2016 | LumosLearning.com

10. What is the appropriate way to cite the following information?

It was a dark and stormy night. The people of Cape Hatteras hid indoors. Mrs. Peabody shivered, hoping the hurricane would not visit and wondering whether she would be able to fall asleep. Across the street, Mr. Greer kept watch from the high tower of his attic, certain that the hurricane would strike soon.

- Ⓐ The newspaper reported on the hurricane. The writer explained, "The people of Cape Hatteras hid indoors. ... Mr. Greer kept watch from the high tower of his attic...."
- Ⓑ The newspaper reported on the hurricane. The writer explained, "The people of Cape Hatteras hid indoors; Mr. Greer kept watch from the high tower of his attic...."
- Ⓒ The newspaper reported on the hurricane. The writer explained, "The people of Cape Hatteras hid indoors. Mr. Greer kept watch from the high tower of his attic...."
- Ⓓ none of the above

© Lumos Information Services 2016 | LumosLearning.com

Lesson 9: Spelling (L8.2.C)

1. **What are homophones or homonyms?**

   Ⓐ the scientific name for humans
   Ⓑ two or more words that are pronounced the same but have different meanings
   Ⓒ two or more words that mean the opposite
   Ⓓ none of the above

2. **Choose the words that correctly complete the following sentence. Make sure that you pick the answer that shows the words in the correct sequence, as they would appear in the sentence.**

   I accidentally _____ the ball _____ the living room window.

   Ⓐ through/ threw
   Ⓑ threw/ though
   Ⓒ threw/ through
   Ⓓ through/through

3. **Choose the words that correctly complete the following sentence. Make sure that you pick the answer that shows the words in the correct sequence, as they would appear in the sentence.**

   My cousins are so silly. _____ always running late because _____ are no alarm clocks in _____ house to wake them up in the morning.

   Ⓐ There, they're, their
   Ⓑ They're, there, their
   Ⓒ Their, there, they're
   Ⓓ There, there, there

© Lumos Information Services 2016 | LumosLearning.com

4.   Which word(s) in the following passage are misspelled?

I was trying to acommodate all of my friends. They were all coming to my birthday party, and I wanted to insure that I had the coolest prizes for the winners of the games; I made sure their were enough prizes for everyone.

- (A) acommodate
- (B) insure
- (C) their
- (D) all of the above

5.   Which word(s) in the following passage are misspelled?

The night of the dance was amazing. My parents rented a limousine for my friends and me. When it pulled up, the chaufer held the door open for us and we climbed in, one after the other. We wore the fanciest dresses that we could find and wore the sparkliest accessories.

- (A) limousine
- (B) chaufer
- (C) sparkliest
- (D) accessories

6.   What is the correct spelling for the misspelled or misused word in the sentence below?

I couldn't weight to go to the movies.

- (A) wait
- (B) wieght
- (C) moovies
- (D) moveis

7.   What is the correct spelling for the misspelled word in the sentence below?

I had to write a buisness letter for English class.

- (A) right
- (B) business
- (C) bisness
- (D) english

© Lumos Information Services 2016 | LumosLearning.com

8.   What is the correct spelling for the misspelled word in the sentence below?

Usually, I like to read on the beach; however, occationally I will swim.

- Ⓐ   usualy
- Ⓑ   beech
- Ⓒ   occasionally
- Ⓓ   how ever

9.   What is the correct spelling for the misspelled word in the sentence below?

I am going to perswade my mother to buy me a dog.

- Ⓐ   gowing
- Ⓑ   persuade
- Ⓒ   by
- Ⓓ   mother

10.   What is the correct spelling for the misspelled word in the sentence below?

It is unclear whether or not I will go on vacation with my family.

- Ⓐ   weather
- Ⓑ   knot
- Ⓒ   vacetion
- Ⓓ   uncleer

© Lumos Information Services 2016 | LumosLearning.com

Lesson 10: Mood in Verbs (L.8.3A)

1. **All verbs in the English language have which of the following?**

    Ⓐ mood
    Ⓑ tense
    Ⓒ voice
    Ⓓ all of the above

2. **What of the following is NOT a mood in verbs?**

    Ⓐ active
    Ⓑ subjunctive
    Ⓒ indicative
    Ⓓ imperative

3. **In which of the following instances would the subjunctive mood be necessary?**

    Ⓐ writing about a hypothetical situation
    Ⓑ making a wish
    Ⓒ making a suggestion
    Ⓓ all of the above

4. **What is the mood of a verb?**

    Ⓐ how the author feels before writing
    Ⓑ what state of mind the author is in when writing
    Ⓒ the author's attitude about what he is writing
    Ⓓ none of the above

5. **The indicative mood of a verb does what?**

    Ⓐ gives a command
    Ⓑ states a fact
    Ⓒ expresses a wish
    Ⓓ states a condition

6. **The imperative mood of a verb does what?**

    Ⓐ gives a command
    Ⓑ states a fact
    Ⓒ expresses a wish
    Ⓓ states a condition

7. **The subjunctive mood of a verb does what?**

    Ⓐ gives a command
    Ⓑ states a fact
    Ⓒ expresses a wish
    Ⓓ states a condition

8. **Which of the following sentences is written in the subjunctive mood?**

    Ⓐ It will rain tomorrow.
    Ⓑ It might rain tomorrow.
    Ⓒ Prepare for the rain tomorrow.
    Ⓓ none of the above

9. **Which of the following sentences is written in the imperative mood?**

    Ⓐ It will rain tomorrow.
    Ⓑ It might rain tomorrow.
    Ⓒ Prepare for the rain tomorrow.
    Ⓓ none of the above

10. **Which of the following sentences is written in the indicative mood?**

    Ⓐ It will rain tomorrow.
    Ⓑ It might rain tomorrow.
    Ⓒ Prepare for the rain tomorrow.
    Ⓓ none of the above

© Lumos Information Services 2016 | LumosLearning.com

Lesson 11: Context Clues (L.8.4.A)

1. **The context of a word means** _____.

    Ⓐ the words that surround it
    Ⓑ words that don't mean the same as they say
    Ⓒ using detail
    Ⓓ finding facts to support

2. **What should you do when using context clues?**

    Ⓐ Read the sentence containing the unfamiliar word, leaving that word out.
    Ⓑ Look closely at the words around the unfamiliar word to help guess its meaning.
    Ⓒ Substitute a possible meaning for the word and read the sentence to see if it makes sense.
    Ⓓ all of the above

3. **Brian appeared infallible on the basketball court because he never missed a shot.**

    What is the best meaning of infallible?

    Ⓐ incapable of making an error
    Ⓑ imperfect
    Ⓒ faulty
    Ⓓ unsure of what he's doing

4. **After the police broke up a skirmish between opposing groups, everyone went their separate ways.**

    What is the best meaning of skirmish?

    Ⓐ peace protest
    Ⓑ fight
    Ⓒ theft
    Ⓓ agreement

5.   **What is the best meaning of excruciating?**

    Ⓐ   bearable

    Ⓑ   extremely pleasant

    Ⓒ   unbearable

    Ⓓ   soon went away

6.   **Michael's overt flirting with Michelle during lunch drew the attention of Larry, her boyfriend.**

What is the best meaning of overt?

    Ⓐ   concealed

    Ⓑ   hidden

    Ⓒ   obvious

    Ⓓ   secret

7.   **Vanity got the best of Sarah as she ran into the wall while checking her hair in the mirror at the end of the hallway.**

What is the best meaning of vanity?

    Ⓐ   modestly

    Ⓑ   pride in one's qualities

    Ⓒ   lack of real value

    Ⓓ   tried things in vain

8.   **Becca's rude and pithy response to her teacher only took a second, but it landed her a week in after school detention.**

What is the best meaning of pithy?

    Ⓐ   brief

    Ⓑ   long winded

    Ⓒ   sweet

    Ⓓ   impolite

© Lumos Information Services 2016 | LumosLearning.com

9. **His emotions were difficult to articulate, but Fredrick knew it was now or never. He had to tell Francie how much he loved her before she got on the bus and left him and his heart forever.**

What is the best meaning for the word articulate?

- Ⓐ unclear
- Ⓑ clearly spoken
- Ⓒ hidden
- Ⓓ move in segments

10. **The pungent odor of my mom's shower cleaning fluid burned my nostrils and made it hard for me to breathe.**

What is the best meaning of pungent?

- Ⓐ pleasant
- Ⓑ bland
- Ⓒ sharp or acidy
- Ⓓ odorless

Lesson 12: Multiple Meaning Words (L.8.4.B)

1. **What is a homonym?**

    Ⓐ words that sound the same but have different meanings and spellings
    Ⓑ words that sound the same and have the same spelling but different meaning
    Ⓒ words that do not sound the same or have the same spelling or meaning
    Ⓓ words that neither sound or look alike

2. **What is the correct definition of a homophone?**

    Ⓐ words that sound and look alike
    Ⓑ words that sound alike but are spelled differently
    Ⓒ words that sound different but mean the same thing
    Ⓓ none of the above

3. **Choose the set of words that are synonyms for "graduation."**

    Ⓐ confidence, realize, concentration
    Ⓑ completion, commencement, closure
    Ⓒ completion, intention, concentration
    Ⓓ completion, culmination, close

4. **Which meaning of the word "address" is used in the following sentence?**

    One should always address the president as, "Mr. President".

    Ⓐ a formal communication
    Ⓑ a place where a person or organization can be contacted
    Ⓒ to direct a speech
    Ⓓ the place you live

5. Which of the homophones, "complement" and "compliment," will correctly fit into the following sentence?

I like to wear my blue, flowered dress. Whenever I wear it I receive a lot of _____ (s).

- (A) compliment
- (B) complement

6. Which meaning of the word "strike" is used in the following sentence?

If the two sides cannot come to an agreement, there will be a strike.

- (A) to aim and deliver a blow
- (B) to lower a flag, as in surrender
- (C) to knock all the pins down in bowling
- (D) to stop work in an attempt to force an employer to comply with demands

7. Choose the word that is a synonym for the underlined word in the following sentence.

Amanda has not been feeling well lately. She went to visit her doctor today to _determine_ why she has been under the weather.

- (A) settle
- (B) decline
- (C) abstain
- (D) study

8. What is the correct definition of the word "suit" as it is used in the sentence below?

When I decided not to go to the prom, my girlfriend said, "Suit yourself. I'll find someone else to dance with."

- (A) formal attire
- (B) legal action
- (C) benefit
- (D) request

© Lumos Information Services 2016 | LumosLearning.com

9.   What is the correct definition of the word "band" as it is used in the sentence below?

Let's band together to stamp out hunger!

    Ⓐ encircle

    Ⓑ a group of people with the same interest

    Ⓒ to come together

    Ⓓ a musical group

10.   What is the correct definition of the word "fair" as it is used in the sentence below?

I couldn't wait for the fair to come to town. Nothing beats a funnel cake from the fair!

    Ⓐ impartial

    Ⓑ a carnival

    Ⓒ equal

    Ⓓ a charge for transportation

© Lumos Information Services 2016 | LumosLearning.com

Lesson 13: Roots, Affixes, and Syllables (L.8.4.B)

1. **Where does the prefix go in a word?**

    Ⓐ at the end
    Ⓑ at the beginning
    Ⓒ in the middle
    Ⓓ none of the above

2. **Where does a suffix go in a word?**

    Ⓐ at the end
    Ⓑ at the beginning
    Ⓒ in the middle
    Ⓓ none of the above

3. **What is an affix?**

    Ⓐ a repair for something
    Ⓑ a prefix or suffix attached to a root to form a new word
    Ⓒ a sound made by blends of letters
    Ⓓ the phonetic understanding of words

4. **What is the best definition of a "root" of a word?**

    Ⓐ the beginning of a word
    Ⓑ the end of a word
    Ⓒ the base of a word
    Ⓓ the middle of the word

5. **What is a syllable?**

    Ⓐ the sound of a vowel when pronouncing a word
    Ⓑ what a teacher gives students that outlines what will be studied in class
    Ⓒ the sound of a consonant when pronouncing a word
    Ⓓ a prefix or suffix attached to a root to form a new word

6.   **An omnivore is an animal that eats both plants and meat. What does the prefix omni mean?**

   Ⓐ   everywhere or everything
   Ⓑ   animal
   Ⓒ   to eat
   Ⓓ   starvation

7.   **Identify the affixes in the following words?**

mislead, unrestricted, reiterate

   Ⓐ   mis, un, re
   Ⓑ   lead, ed, ate
   Ⓒ   lead, stricted, rate
   Ⓓ   lead, restricted, iterate

8.   **The root word, cede means, "to go". With this knowledge, determine the meaning of the word, "precede".**

   Ⓐ   to go after
   Ⓑ   to go away
   Ⓒ   to go before
   Ⓓ   to go never

9.   **Dynamic means physical force or energy. What does the root word "dyna" means?**

   Ⓐ   to be weak
   Ⓑ   power
   Ⓒ   to be little
   Ⓓ   to be tired

10.   **The prefix "un" means not. What does "unable" mean?**

   Ⓐ   ready
   Ⓑ   not able
   Ⓒ   unclear
   Ⓓ   not unable

© Lumos Information Services 2016 | LumosLearning.com

Lesson 14: Reference Materials (L.8.4.C)

1.   Which of the following are acceptable reference materials to use for a research assignment?

Ⓐ   questionnaires
Ⓑ   experiments
Ⓒ   field studies
Ⓓ   scholarly articles
Ⓔ   all of the above

2.   What are primary sources?

Ⓐ   materials that come directly from the source
Ⓑ   materials that have been copied from the source
Ⓒ   materials that are found only in encyclopedias
Ⓓ   materials that are over 100 years old

3.   Which of the following are examples of secondary sources?

Ⓐ   biographies
Ⓑ   encyclopedias
Ⓒ   textbooks
Ⓓ   documentaries
Ⓔ   all of the above

4.   How can you determine whether a source is reliable?

Ⓐ   If you obtained your information from the Internet, it is always reliable.
Ⓑ   You should consider who wrote the source and why.
Ⓒ   If you obtained your information from an actual article, it will be reliable.
Ⓓ   answer choices B & C

5.   Why must you be very careful about obtaining information from websites?

- Ⓐ   It can be difficult to find reputable sources.
- Ⓑ   Some sites can be edited by anyone.
- Ⓒ   It is too easy to find what may look like good information but sources are often unverifiable.
- Ⓓ   all of the above

6.   What are the benefits of using primary sources?

- Ⓐ   They are first-hand accounts from those who witnessed or experienced the event being researched.
- Ⓑ   They offer a limited perspective.
- Ⓒ   They haven't been very well researched.
- Ⓓ   They are reposted hundreds of times.

7.   What are the benefits of using secondary sources?

- Ⓐ   They have been analyzed and interpreted.
- Ⓑ   They have not often used a variety of primary sources to come to their conclusions.
- Ⓒ   They are straight from the source.
- Ⓓ   They have been reposted hundreds of times.

8.   What do the following items have in common?

diary

journal

letter

official letters

- Ⓐ   They are secondary sources.
- Ⓑ   They are primary sources.
- Ⓒ   They are neither primary nor secondary sources.

© Lumos Information Services 2016 | LumosLearning.com

Name: _____ **Date:** _____

9. **What do the following items have in common?**

books

journal articles

textbooks

reference sources

- Ⓐ They are primary sources.
- Ⓑ They are secondary sources.
- Ⓒ Some are secondary sources.
- Ⓓ none of the above

10. **If you were researching Anne Frank, which of the following would be your choice for a primary source?**

- Ⓐ your teacher
- Ⓑ an encyclopedia
- Ⓒ a website about Anne Frank
- Ⓓ Anne Frank's diary

© Lumos Information Services 2016 | LumosLearning.com

Lesson 15: Using Context to Verify Meaning (L.8.4.D)

Marathon

Training for a marathon takes hard work and **perseverance**. It is not something you can do on the **spur** of the moment. Preparing for a marathon takes months, particularly if you have never run a marathon before. The official distance of a full marathon is 26.2 miles. In 2005, the average time to complete a marathon in the United States was 4 hours 32 minutes 8 seconds for men and 5 hours 6 minutes 8 seconds for women.

Most people who run marathons are not trying to win. Many runners try to beat their own best time. Some compare their time to other runners in the same gender and age group. Some people set time-oriented goals, such as finishing under four hours, while others try to complete the race without slowing to a walk. Many beginners simply hope to finish the marathon.

Trainers recommend that beginners maintain a **consistent** running schedule for six weeks prior to even starting a marathon training program. The purpose of this is to allow the body to adapt to the **various** physical demands of long distance running. First-time marathon runners should train by running four days a week for at least four months, increasing distance by no more than ten percent weekly. As race day approaches, runners should **taper** their runs, reducing the strain on their bodies and resting before the marathon. It is important not to over **exert** yourself during training because that can lead to lot of injuries. Most common injuries are spraining of the knees and ankles. These sprains can **hinder** the training.

Before the race, it is important to stretch in order to keep muscles **limber**. Staying hydrated is also important, but there is a danger in drinking too much water. If a runner drinks too much water, they may experience a dangerous condition called **hyponatremia**, a drop of sodium levels in the blood. During the race, trainers recommend maintaining a steady pace. It is normal to feel sore after a marathon. Light exercise will help sore muscles heal faster.

Some people run marathons in pairs or groups. Training for and running a marathon with another person or group of people can make the experience more enjoyable and more rewarding. A running partner might be just the motivation you need to show up for an early morning run instead of rolling over to hit the snooze button. And, when you cross the finish line together, you can share the satisfaction of reaching your common goal.

Usually, thousands of people sign up and run a marathon. Most people finish the race. The thrill of running a marathon for the first time is unbelievable. The training sessions are harder if you have never run before. But it is unbelievable what ones' body can do when one puts his/her mind to it. Having a good coach to support you makes all the difference in training for a marathon.

© Lumos Information Services 2016 | LumosLearning.com

The daily runs are very important. Strength training and core training are also very important.

Using context clues in the story determine the meaning of the bold words.

1.   perseverance

    Ⓐ determination

    Ⓑ routine

    Ⓒ flexibility

    Ⓓ practice

2.   spur

    Ⓐ after long planning

    Ⓑ without planning

    Ⓒ with much discussion

    Ⓓ with significant thought

3.   consistent

    Ⓐ varying

    Ⓑ changing

    Ⓒ regular

    Ⓓ dynamic

4.   various

    Ⓐ many

    Ⓑ few

    Ⓒ hard

    Ⓓ simple

5.   taper

    Ⓐ add more

    Ⓑ pick and choose

    Ⓒ scale back

    Ⓓ candle

© Lumos Information Services 2016 | LumosLearning.com

Name: ___ Date: ___

6. **exert**

   Ⓐ sleep
   Ⓑ utilize
   Ⓒ rest
   Ⓓ run

7. **hinder**

   Ⓐ delay
   Ⓑ speed up
   Ⓒ help
   Ⓓ assist

8. **limber**

   Ⓐ tone
   Ⓑ tight
   Ⓒ loose
   Ⓓ wavy

9. **hyponatremia**

   Ⓐ a drop of sodium levels in the blood
   Ⓑ dehydration
   Ⓒ a pulled muscle
   Ⓓ easily able to swim

10. **If you cannot determine a word's meaning in context, where can you look?**

    Ⓐ thesaurus
    Ⓑ dictionary
    Ⓒ encyclopedia
    Ⓓ journal

© Lumos Information Services 2016 | LumosLearning.com

Lesson 16: Interpreting Figures of Speech (L.8.5.A)

1.   How is a metaphor different than a simile?

Ⓐ   A metaphor is the same as a simile.

Ⓑ   A metaphor does not use like or as in the comparison of two unlike things.

Ⓒ   A metaphor is not at all similar to a simile.

Ⓓ   A metaphor uses like or as in the comparison of two unlike things.

2.   What two figures of speech listed below have to do with word sounds?

Ⓐ   metaphor and simile

Ⓑ   personification and idiom

Ⓒ   alliteration and onomatopoeia

Ⓓ   noun and verb

3.   Which of the following is a metaphor?

Ⓐ   It is as hot as the surface of the sun out there.

Ⓑ   She sold seashells by the seashore.

Ⓒ   I stayed up too late last night studying and now my mind is foggy.

Ⓓ   She plopped on the sofa after babysitting nine hours.

4.   What does the idiom, burning the candle at both ends mean?

Ⓐ   You are wasting wax.

Ⓑ   You are doing too much.

Ⓒ   You are preparing for an emergency.

Ⓓ   You have a great need for a lot of light.

5.   What is the meaning of the following simile?

Her eyes are like fiery diamonds.

Ⓐ   sparkly and bright

Ⓑ   hard and hot

Ⓒ   warm and light

Ⓓ   expensive and desirable

6. **Today, my brother and I went to the batting cages. I was in awe of him as I watched him hit ball after ball; he was a machine.**

Why is the brother being compared to a machine?

Ⓐ He seemed to be under the control of a robot.
Ⓑ He hit every ball with accuracy and efficiency.
Ⓒ He was rigid and metal-like.
Ⓓ He didn't show much emotion as he hit the balls.

7. **What is the meaning of the following metaphor?**

He has the heart of a lion.

Ⓐ the people on the street
Ⓑ He is hairy.
Ⓒ He has a large heart.
Ⓓ He is courageous.

8. **What figure of speech is used in the following sentence?**

The leaves of the tree danced in the breeze.

Ⓐ personification
Ⓑ metaphor
Ⓒ simile
Ⓓ idiom

9. **Donna's brother said, "you're selling yourself short." What does she mean by this?**

Ⓐ you need to grow a little taller
Ⓑ you are not giving yourself enough credit
Ⓒ you are a little short
Ⓓ you do not need to worry about being tall

© Lumos Information Services 2016 | LumosLearning.com

10. What figure of speech is used in the following sentence?

I saw the coolest concert last night.

- Ⓐ personification
- Ⓑ alliteration
- Ⓒ metaphor
- Ⓓ simile

Lesson 17: Relationships Between Words (L.8.5.B)

1. **What is an analogy?**

    Ⓐ   words that mean the opposite
    Ⓑ   a comparison of two words
    Ⓒ   a short story
    Ⓓ   the study of ants

2. **Select the best choice to explain the relationship of the words in the following analogy.**

    branch is to tree as fingers are to hand

    Ⓐ   antonyms
    Ⓑ   synonyms
    Ⓒ   part to whole
    Ⓓ   whole to part

3. **Select the best choice to finish the following analogy.**

    repel is to attract as _____ is to lead

    Ⓐ   follow
    Ⓑ   guide
    Ⓒ   direct
    Ⓓ   head

4. **Select the best choice to finish the following analogy.**

    I is to mine as they is to _____

    Ⓐ   there's
    Ⓑ   theirs
    Ⓒ   they'res
    Ⓓ   theirses

© Lumos Information Services 2016 | LumosLearning.com

5.   Select the best choice to finish the following analogy.

ostracism is to acceptance as _____ is to charitable

- (A) deliberate
- (B) rejection
- (C) greedy
- (D) giving

6.   Study the analogy below to determine the relationship between the words that are presented.

won is to one as rode is to road

- (A) homonyms
- (B) synonyms
- (C) homophones
- (D) homographs

7.   Study the analogy below to determine the relationship between the words that are presented.

woman is to women as mouse is to mice

- (A) present tense to past tense
- (B) singular to plural
- (C) plural to singular
- (D) antonyms

8.   Finish the following analogy.

tiny is to small as enormous is to

- (A) minute
- (B) monstrous
- (C) large
- (D) petite

9. **Complete the following analogy.**

television is to view as _____ is to listen

- Ⓐ radio
- Ⓑ movie
- Ⓒ computer
- Ⓓ people

10. **Finish the following analogy.**

woman is to girl as man is to _____

- Ⓐ son
- Ⓑ boy
- Ⓒ father
- Ⓓ dad

© Lumos Information Services 2016 | LumosLearning.com

Lesson 18: Denotations and Connotations (L.8.5.C)

1. **The denotation of a word is the literal dictionary definition. The connotation of a word is the idea or feeling associated with the word.**

Is the underlined word used denotatively or connotatively?

That girl is <u>immature</u> and impossible to be around because she is always goofing around and is a huge disruption in class.

Ⓐ   denotatively
Ⓑ   connotatively
Ⓒ   both

2. **Which of the following words has the most positive connotation?**

dwelling, house, home, residence

Ⓐ   dwelling
Ⓑ   house
Ⓒ   home
Ⓓ   residence

3. **Which of the following words has the most negative connotation?**

cheap, frugal, thrifty

Ⓐ   cheap
Ⓑ   frugal
Ⓒ   thrifty

4. **Which of the following has the most positive connotation?**

Ⓐ   plain
Ⓑ   dull
Ⓒ   ugly
Ⓓ   unattractive

5.   Which word has the most neutral connotation?

assertive, pushy, aggressive

    Ⓐ   assertive
    Ⓑ   pushy
    Ⓒ   aggressive

6.   What is a negative connotation for funny?

    Ⓐ   absurd
    Ⓑ   uncommon
    Ⓒ   comical
    Ⓓ   amusing

7.   What would a negative connotation for the word "quick" be?

    Ⓐ   prompt
    Ⓑ   rapid
    Ⓒ   hasty
    Ⓓ   responsive

8.   What is a neutral connotation for small?

    Ⓐ   short
    Ⓑ   paltry
    Ⓒ   insignificant
    Ⓓ   trivial

9.   My mom screamed when she realized she won first place in the pie baking contest.

Does the word "screamed" in the above sentence have a positive, negative, or neutral connotation?

    Ⓐ   positive
    Ⓑ   negative
    Ⓒ   neutral

© Lumos Information Services 2016 | LumosLearning.com

10.   My mom screamed as she fell off the ladder into the bushes.

Does the word "screamed" in the above sentence have a positive, negative, or neutral connotation?

- Ⓐ   positive
- Ⓑ   negative
- Ⓒ   neutral

Lesson 19: Domain Specific Words (L.8.6)

1. **What is jargon?**

   Ⓐ words that are silly
   Ⓑ words that are specific to an area a study
   Ⓒ words that are slang
   Ⓓ words that describe nouns

2. **Given the task to write an essay about literature, what would be a good domain specific vocabulary word to use?**

   Ⓐ plot
   Ⓑ characterization
   Ⓒ dialogue
   Ⓓ all of the above

3. **Read the passage below; identify a domain specific vocabulary word in it.**

   After reading the novel, it is clear that the author's use of setting is meant a symbol for bravery.

   Ⓐ symbol
   Ⓑ bravery
   Ⓒ use
   Ⓓ author's

4. **Which of the following words would best fit in the following sentence?**

   Samuel felt _____ by his teachers consistent nagging about his grades. He knew he needed to bring them up, and her constant reminders increased his anxiety.

   Ⓐ angry
   Ⓑ annoyed
   Ⓒ frustrated
   Ⓓ mad

© Lumos Information Services 2016 | LumosLearning.com

5.   What word in the following sentence is a domain specific vocabulary word?

An animal's predatory instincts are what helps it survive when it needs food or protection.

    Ⓐ   instinct

    Ⓑ   animal

    Ⓒ   food

    Ⓓ   protection

6.   What word in the following sentence is a domain specific vocabulary word?

The slope of the line is calculated using slope intercept form. It is important to understand this formula if you want to be a successful math student.

    Ⓐ   student

    Ⓑ   successful

    Ⓒ   calculated

    Ⓓ   important

7.   What word in the following sentence is a domain specific vocabulary word?

The economy is governed by supply and demand. The market is what drives the economy and the economy is what capitalism is based upon.

    Ⓐ   market

    Ⓑ   economy

    Ⓒ   capitalism

    Ⓓ   all of the above

8.   What word in the following sentence is a domain specific vocabulary word?

The poem can be interpreted in many ways. Readers can begin their interpretation by looking at a poem's meter, and then by closely examining its rhyme scheme and its rhythm. The overall interpretation should include the many nuances of the poem.

    Ⓐ   interpreted

    Ⓑ   meter

    Ⓒ   nuances

    Ⓓ   closely

© Lumos Information Services 2016 | LumosLearning.com

9.   **What word in the following sentence is a domain specific vocabulary word?**

Look closely to see that the plugs and plug wires are all in good shape. Do this simple check before taking your car to the mechanic and it might save you a few bucks. Keep your money in your pocket if you can.

     Ⓐ   plugs

     Ⓑ   check

     Ⓒ   mechanic

     Ⓓ   pocket

10.   **What word in the following sentence is a domain specific vocabulary word?**

Check the motherboard first. If the motherboard is fried, you might as well just go to the store and get a new computer. There is no sense in spending that much time and energy to fix your machine if the brain of it is broken.

     Ⓐ   motherboard

     Ⓑ   fried

     Ⓒ   sense

     Ⓓ   broken

End of Language

© Lumos Information Services 2016 | LumosLearning.com

Language

Answer Key
&
Detailed Explanations

© Lumos Information Services 2016 | LumosLearning.com

Lesson 1: Adjectives and Adverbs (L.8.1.A)

Question	Answer	Detailed Explanation
1.	B	Answer choice B is correct. An adjective describes or modifies a noun in a sentence..
2.	D	Answer choice D is correct. An adverb can modify an adjective, verb, or another adverb in a sentence.
3.	D	Answer choice D is correct. The word "good" is an adjective that is used to describe a person, place, thing, or idea. The word "well" is an adverb that is used to explain how something is done.
4.	C	Answer choice C is correct. In the first sentence, the word "bad" is an adverb describing how the narrator felt. In the second sentence, the word "well" is an adverb describing how the narrator did on a test. In the third sentence, the word "honestly" is an adverb describing how a question was answered.
5.	A	Answer choice A is correct. The word "patiently" is an adverb describing how Miss Jenkins teaches.
6.	D	Answer choice D is correct. The words "very" and "carefully" are both adverbs which describe how the baby was picked up.
7.	D	Answer choice D is correct. The adjectives "tired, dirty, and hungry" describe how the narrator feels after a long afternoon at practice.
8.	A	Answer choice A is correct. The word "pretty" is used to describe the girl. The adjective is describing the noun in this sentence.
9.	A	Answer choice A is correct. The adverb is "slowly." It describes how the man walked.
10.	A	Answer choice A is correct. The word "sadly" describes how the narrator walked after a tough baseball game.

© Lumos Information Services 2016 | LumosLearning.com

Lesson 2: Subject-Verb Agreement (L.8.1.B)

Question	Answer	Detailed Explanation
1.	B	Answer choice B is correct. When subjects are connected by "or", the subject closest to the verb determines whether the verb is plural or singular.
2.	A	Answer choice A is correct. When there is more than one subject, where one is singular and the other is plural (cat and dogs), the verb (have) will match the subject that is closest to it. So, if the sentence was written as, "Neither the dogs nor the cat...", the verb would be "has" because the subject "cat" is singular. The sentence would read like this, "Neither the dogs nor the cat has been fed".
3.	A	Answer choice A is correct. When subject are connected by "or", the subject closest to the verb determines whether the verb is plural or singular.
4.	B	Answer choice B is correct. This is a tricky sentence. The word "some" is not the subject, "answers" is. Because the subject is plural, we use the plural form of the verb, which is "seem."
5.	B	Answer choice B is correct. When the subject has two or more nouns connected by "and", use a plural verb.
6.	A	Answer choice A is correct. When two or more singular nouns are connected with "or" or "nor" use a singular verb.
7.	A	Answer choice A is correct. The subject of this sentence is "the student," which is singular, so the verb must also be singular. Be careful with sentences that put a phrase in between the subject and the verb.
8.	A	Answer choice A is correct. When there is more than one subject, one being singular and one being plural, the verb matches the subject closest to it.
9.	B	Answer choice B is correct. "Food" is the subject of the sentence.
10.	C	Answer choice C is correct. There are two subjects in this sentence.

© Lumos Information Services 2016 | LumosLearning.com

Lesson 3: Pronouns (L.8.1.C)

Question	Answer	Detailed Explanation
1.	B	Answer choice B is correct. When a pronoun and a noun are used together, choose the pronoun that would fit best if the noun were not there. Answer choice A is incorrect because "we" would not fit without the noun students.
2.	A	Answer choice A is correct. "I" is the correct answer. One way to test whether you have the correct answer is to write the sentence out using only the pronoun you are testing and the object. For example, to test the word, "I", you would write, "I enjoyed spending the day at the fair". In contrast, if you were to test the word, "me" you would write, "Me enjoyed spending the day at the fair". This is not correct.
3.	A	Answer choice A is correct. When a pronoun and a noun are used together, choose the pronoun that would fit best if the noun were not there.
4.	A	Answer choice A is correct. That, this, these, those, and such are demonstrative pronouns which means they identify or point to nouns. They can even convey emotion.
5.	A	Answer choice A is correct. The correct answer is "who". Who is a subject pronoun and Whom is an object pronoun. The subject of the sentence above is, "The woman" therefore, you use the pronoun, "who" when referring to her. A test to determine which pronoun to use is to substitute the words "who" and "whom", with "she" and "her". Whenever the word "she" is appropriate, the pronoun "who" can be used. Whenever the word "her" is appropriate, the word "whom" can be used. You would apply this to the above sentence, by asking the question, "Who would like to make a reservation?" The answer is, "she would." According to the test, we would use the pronoun "who".
6.	B	Answer choice B is correct. "Who" is a subject pronoun and "whom" is an object pronoun. In the sentence above, the word "you" is the subject, and "whom" is the direct object. A test to determine which pronoun to use is to substitute the words "who" and "whom" with "she" and "her". Whenever the word "she" is appropriate, the pronoun "who" can be used. Whenever the word "her" is appropriate, the word "whom" can be used. You would apply this test to the sentence by asking the question, "Who am I speaking with?" To which the answer would be, "I am speaking with her". According to the test, we would use the pronoun, "whom".

© Lumos Information Services 2016 | LumosLearning.com

Question	Answer	Detailed Explanation
7.	B	Answer choice B is correct. Who is a subject pronoun and whom is an object pronoun. The subject of the sentence above is you, so we know that the answer is whom because it is the direct object. A test to determine which pronoun to use is to substitute the words who and whom with she and her. Whenever the word she is appropriate, the pronoun who can be used. Whenever the word her can be used, the pronoun whom can be used. You would apply this to the sentence above by answering the question which is being asked. The answer would be, "They are sending her to help us". According to the test we would use the pronoun, whom.
8.	D	Answer choice D is correct. The pronoun "her" is used three times and refers to Martha.
9.	B	Answer choice B is correct. The demonstrative pronoun "those" conveys disdain for the choice of shoes.
10.	C	Answer choice C is correct. The pronoun "him" refers to Mike. If the noun, Mike, were repeated, the sentence would read: Mike's mother told Mike that the trash needed to be taken out sooner rather than later. Using pronouns makes our writing clearer and less repetitive.

Lesson 4: Phrases and Clauses (L.8.1.C)

Question	Answer	Detailed Explanation
1.	A	Answer choice A is correct. An infinitive phrase always begins with the word "to" followed by a verb. In this case, the infinitive phrase in the sentence is "To make my birthday special."
2.	A	Answer choice A is correct. It is an independent clause because it can stand alone.
3.	B	Answer choice B is correct. A subordinate, also called a dependent, clause depends on more words in the sentence. It cannot stand alone and always begins with a subordinate conjunction or a relative pronoun.
4.	A	Answer choice A is correct. It is an independent clause because it can stand alone.
5.	B	Answer choice B is correct. A subordinate, also called a dependent, clause depends on more words in the sentence. It cannot stand alone and always begins with a subordinate conjunction or a relative pronoun.
6.	A	Answer choice A is correct. An independent clause has a subject and a verb and can stand by itself.
7.	B	Answer choice B is correct. A subordinate clause, also known as a dependent clause, has a subject and a verb but cannot stand by itself as a complete sentence.
8.	C	Answer choice C is correct. An adjective phrase modifies a noun and tells "what kind" or "which one."
9.	B	Answer choice B is correct. The adjective phrase is "with the bright blue collar." It describes (tells which one) the dog.
10.	B	Answer choice B is correct. The adverb clause is "because she did not clean her room." Adverb phrases are dependent, meaning they cannot stand alone.

© Lumos Information Services 2016 | LumosLearning.com

Lesson 5: Verbals (L.8.1.D)

Question	Answer	Detailed Explanation
1.	B	Answer choice B is correct. A verbal is a verb that acts as another part of speech, such as an adjective or verb.
2.	B	Answer choice B is correct. A participle is a verbal that functions as an adjective and will end with either an -ing, -en, or -ed.
3.	B	Answer choice B is correct. Gerunds take the place of nouns in a sentence, and they are made by adding -ing to the original verb.
4.	B	Answer choice B is correct. Infinitives are usually marked with the word "to" followed by a verb.
5.	B	Answer choice B is correct. Infinitives use the word "to" followed by a verb; in this case, the infinitive is "to visit."
6.	A	Answer choice A is correct. While there are two sentences that include a verbal ending in -ing, the gerund is the one that takes the place of a noun.
7.	B	Answer choice B is correct. The participle, "boiling on the stove," describes the soup.
8.	B	Answer choice B is correct. The word "sparkling" describes the ring; therefore, it works as an adjective in this sentence.
9.	C	Answer choice C is correct. The word "sleeping" functions as a verb in the sentence.
10.	B	Answer choice B is correct. The word "running" describes the water; therefore, it is functioning as an adjective.

© Lumos Information Services 2016 | LumosLearning.com

Lesson 6: Active and Passive Voice (L.8.3.A)

Question	Answer	Detailed Explanation
1.	A	Answer choice A is correct. The subject comes before the action in active voice.
2.	D	Answer choice D is correct. A sentence written in the passive voice means the subject is acted upon instead of doing the action.
3.	C	Answer choice C is correct. A sentence written in active voice means the subject of the sentence is performing the action.
4.	B	Answer choice B is correct. The correct answer is passive. When the voice is active, the subject is doing the action. When the voice is passive, the target or object is treated like the subject of the sentence. In the sentence above, the subject is Brian, but Margaret is being treated like the subject.
5.	B	Answer choice B is correct. The correct answer is passive because the subject of the sentence, which is Matthew, is being treated as the object. We know that Matthew is the subject because he is doing the action.
6.	A	Answer choice A is correct. The correct answer is active. The subject of the sentence is Samantha, as she is doing the action, and she is treated as the subject. If this sentence were passive it would read, "The wedding dress was sewn by Samantha." The answer could not be neither, because a sentence is ALWAYS either active or passive.
7.	B	Answer choice B is correct. Both B and C are written in active voice. The sentences show that the subjects are doing the action.
8.	D	Answer choice D is correct. Both of the above sentences are written in passive voice. In both examples, the objects are being treated as the subject.
9.	D	Answer choice D is correct. In each of the three sentences, the subject is doing the action, which classifies them as active.
10.	A	The correct answer is A. The subject is being acted upon, instead of doing the action.

© Lumos Information Services 2016 | LumosLearning.com

Lesson 7: Punctuation (L.8.2.A)

Question	Answer	Detailed Explanation
1.	A	Answer choice A is correct. Commas are used to separate three or more items in a list.
2.	C	Answer choice C is correct. When an appositive is in the middle of a sentence, it must be set off by commas. An appositive is a noun phrase that renames or clarifies the noun.
3.	B	Answer choice B is correct. In complex sentences, a subordinating clause is set off with a comma. "After you have finished taking out the trash" is the subordinating clause in the sentence.
4.	C	Answer choice C is correct. A semicolon can separate two closely related independent clauses that are not joined by a coordinating conjunction.
5.	A	Answer choice A is correct. When a singular noun ends in "s" an apostrophe "s" is added to the word. For example, Mrs. Jones's.
6.	C	Answer choice C is correct. In order to make a plural noun possessive, add an apostrophe to the word. If the plural noun does not end with an s, add an apostrophe then an s. Examples include women's, children's and men's.
7.	A	Answer choice A is correct. Commas should be used to separate a series of words or word groups, between two independent clauses joined by a coordinating conjunction (and, or, but, for, nor), and in a date between the day and year. These are not all the comma rules, but they are the rules that are mostly commonly broken.
8.	B	Answer choice B is correct. The missing, or omitted, letters are "h" and "a". The word "would've" is a contraction for the words "would have".
9.	B	Answer choice B is correct. Both names are possessive; a colon is used because a list follows, and commas separate the list.
10.	C	Answer choice C is correct. The dash takes the place of a semicolon in this example. Remember to use dashes sparingly and not in formal writing.

© Lumos Information Services 2016 | LumosLearning.com

Lesson 8: Ellipsis (L.8.2.B)

Question	Answer	Detailed Explanation
1.	A	Answer choice A is correct. An ellipsis is ...
2.	D	Answer choice D is correct. An ellipsis is used to: * Indicating omissions in quoted material * Indicating hesitation or trailing off in spoken words * Imparting extra significance to a sentence
3.	A	Answer choice A is correct. An ellipsis can be used to create suspense.
4.	B	Answer choice B is correct. You can use an ellipsis at any point in a sentence.
5.	A	Answer choice A is correct. The statement above is true.
6.	A	Answer choice A is correct. An ellipsis in dialogue can indicate a pause.
7.	D	Answer choice D is correct. In all of the above examples, an ellipsis would be used.
8.	C	Answer choice C is correct. The ellipsis indicates that information has been omitted.
9.	A	Answer choice A is correct. When you omit the beginning of a sentence: you have to put anything you change in brackets.
10.	A	Answer choice A is correct. The ellipsis indicates that areas of the text have been omitted.

© Lumos Information Services 2016 | LumosLearning.com

Lesson 9: Spelling (L8.2.C)

Question	Answer	Detailed Explanation
1.	B	Answer choice B is correct. Homophones, also known as homonyms, are words that are pronounced the same, but have different meanings. Often they are spelled differently, and it is important to learn to use the correct spelling of the word. An example is: threw, through
2.	C	Answer choice C is correct. The word "threw" means to propel or hurl an object. The word "through" means to go in one end and out another.
3.	B	Answer choice B is correct. The first "they're" is a contraction for "they are." The second "there" refers to a location and the third "their" shows possession.
4.	D	Answer choice D is correct. Answer choice A is spelled accommodate. Answer choice B is a homophone; the correct word is ensure. Answer choice C is also a homophone and should be spelled there.
5.	B	Answer choice B is correct. The correct spelling of this word is chauffeur.
6.	A	Answer choice A is correct. Weight and wait are homophones. Weight is a unit of heaviness. Wait means to stop for a bit. Notice that weight does not follow the rule, "i before e except after c." This is why it is important to use a dictionary when unsure of word spellings.
7.	B	Answer choice B is correct. The correct spelling is business.
8.	C	Answer choice C is correct. The correct spelling is occasionally.
9.	B	Answer choice B is correct. The correct spelling is persuade.
10.	D	Answer choice D is correct. No words are misused or misspelled.

© Lumos Information Services 2016 | LumosLearning.com

Lesson 10: Mood in Verbs (L.8.3.A)

Question	Answer	Detailed Explanation
1.	D	Answer choice D is correct. Verbs have mood, tense, and voice.
2.	A	Answer choice A is correct. Active is a voice, not a mood.
3.	A	Answer choice A is correct. Subjunctive mood suggests an unreal situation.
4.	C	Answer choice C is correct. Mood is an author's attitude about his topic.
5.	B	Answer choice B is correct. The indicative mood of a verb indicates some sort of fact.
6.	A	Answer choice A is correct. The imperative tone of a verb gives a command.
7.	C	Answer choice C is correct. The subjunctive form of a verb expresses anything uncertain. Since a wish is uncertain, it is in a subjunctive mood.
8.	B	Answer choice B is correct because it expresses an uncertainty.
9.	C	Answer choice C is correct. An imperative tone gives a command, and answer choice C is giving a command.
10.	A	Answer choice A is correct because an indicative tone indicates a fact.

© Lumos Information Services 2016 | LumosLearning.com

Lesson 11: Context Clues (L.8.4.A)

Question	Answer	Detailed Explanation
1.	A	Answer choice A is correct. Context clues are the words that surround the unknown word. Context clues help the reader determine the meaning of the word.
2.	D	Answer choice D is correct. When faced with an unfamiliar word in a story or passage, it is helpful to go back and reread the surrounding text, both before and after the unfamiliar word. The words and phrases that help the reader determine the meaning of the word are called context clues.
3.	A	Answer choice A is correct. Context clues can be found at the end of the sentence, "...because he never missed a shot." This means he never made a mistake or error.
4.	B	Answer choice B is correct. After the police broke up a skirmish between opposing groups, everyone went their separate ways.
5.	C	Answer choice C is correct. After running into a parked car and then falling off my bike, the pain in my thumb was excruciating.
6.	C	Answer choice C is correct. Michael's overt flirting with Michelle during lunch drew the attention of Larry, her boyfriend.
7.	B	Answer choice B is correct. Vanity got the best of Sarah as she ran into the wall while checking her hair in the mirror at the end of the hallway.
8.	A	Answer choice A is correct. Becca's rude and pithy response to her teacher only took a second, but it landed her a week in after school detention.
9.	B	Answer choice B is correct. His emotions were difficult to articulate, but Fredrick knew it was now or never. He had to tell Francie how much he loved her before she got on the bus and left him and his heart forever.
10.	C	Answer choice C is correct. The pungent odor of my mom's shower cleaning fluid burned my nostrils and made it hard for me to breathe.

Lesson 12: Multiple Meaning Words (L.8.4.B)

Question	Answer	Detailed Explanation
1.	B	Answer choice B is correct. Homonyms are words that are considered multiple-meaning words. They are words that share the same spelling and pronunciation but have a different meaning.
2.	B	Answer choice B is correct. Homophones are words that sound the same but are spelled differently and have different meanings.
3.	D	Answer choice D is correct. Graduation is a homonym, or multiple-meaning word.
4.	C	Answer choice C is correct. Address is a homonym meaning it is a multiple-meaning word.
5.	A	Answer choice A is correct. The definition of compliment is: praise. The definition of complement is: add to in a way that enhances or improves a thing.
6.	D	Answer choice D is correct. Strike is a homonym meaning it is a multiple-meaning word. All the definitions are correct, but in the context of the sentence, only D is correct.
7.	A	Answer choice A is correct. Determine has many meanings, but within the context of the sentence, only A is correct.
8.	C	Answer choice C is correct. Suit, in this case, means benefit, as in benefit or be happy with your own decision.
9.	C	Answer choice C is correct. While all the definitions for band are correct, within the context of this sentence, only answer choice C is correct.
10.	B	Answer choice B is correct. Fair, in the context of this sentence, means a carnival.

© Lumos Information Services 2016 | LumosLearning.com

Lesson 13: Roots, Affixes, and Syllables (L.8.4.B)

Question	Answer	Detailed Explanation
1.	B	Answer B is correct. The prefix "pre" means before; therefore, a prefix goes at the beginning of a word.
2.	A	Answer choice A is correct. A suffix is the letter blend that goes at the end of a word.
3.	B	Answer choice B is correct. An affix is the prefix or suffix that is attached to a root to create a new word.
4.	C	Answer choice C is correct. The root of a word is the base. It is what a prefix or suffix is attached to.
5.	A	Answer choice A is correct. Syllables are the sounds of vowels when you pronounce a word. The word "cheese" has one syllable. The word "chicken" has two syllables. Answer choice B is incorrect. An outline of the school year that a teacher provides is actually called a syllabus.
6.	A	Answer choice A is correct. The prefix omni means everywhere or everything. An omnivore eats everything (meaning plants and meats). Other words with the prefix omni are omniscient (knowing everything) and omnipotent (having unlimited power).
7.	A	Answer choice A is correct. Mis, un, and re are prefixes. Prefixes are also known as affixes. Suffixes are also affixes.
8.	C	Answer choice C is correct. The prefix "pre" means before. If cede means to, then when combined, the word prefix means to go before.
9.	B	Answer choice B is correct. The root word "dyna" means power. Other words that include the root word dyna are: dynamite and dynamo.
10.	B	Answer choice B is correct. Un, meaning not, plus able means not able to. I am unable to attend the party on Friday.

© Lumos Information Services 2016 | LumosLearning.com

Lesson 14: Reference Materials (L.8.4.C)

Question	Answer	Detailed Explanation
1.	E	Answer choice E is correct. Questionnaires, experiments, field studies, and scholarly articles are all acceptable references for research. Using a variety of these resources makes for the most reliable research.
2.	A	Answer choice A is correct. Primary sources are those that come directly from the source.
3.	E	Answer choice E is correct. Secondary sources interpret and analyze primary sources.
4.	B	Answer choice B is correct. It is difficult to determine the reliability of one or two sources. When doing research, it is important to constantly ask yourself who wrote the resources you are using and why were they written? Using several sources for research will prove to be most reliable.
5.	D	Answer choice D is correct. Use caution when using Internet resources. Make sure the author is reliable and the information is current.
6.	A	Answer choice A. The benefit of using a primary source is that the account from the source actually witnessed or experienced the event being researched.
7.	A	Answer choice A is correct. Using secondary sources for research is beneficial because the primary sources have already been analyzed and interpreted.
8.	B	Answer choice B is correct. Although not a complete list of primary sources, these items are generally considered to be primary sources. The researcher, however, must ensure the validity of the documents.
9.	B	Answer choice B is correct. All four items are considered secondary sources. Secondary sources are those items that are not first-hand accounts of events.
10.	D	Answer choice D is correct. Anne Frank's diary was written by her; therefore it is a primary source.

© Lumos Information Services 2016 | LumosLearning.com

Lesson 15: Using Context to Verify Meaning (L.8.4.D)

Question	Answer	Detailed Explanation
1.	A	Answer A is correct. The context clue is a synonym, "hard work" helps determine the meaning.
2.	B	Answer B is correct. The context clues are antonyms, "preparing takes months".
3.	C	Answer choice C is correct. The context clue "maintain" shows it must stay the same.
4.	A	Answer choice A is correct. Because the context says "demands" not "demand" readers know there are many.
5.	C	Answer choice C is correct. Some of the words in context like "reducing" and "relaxing" show readers that "taper" means to scale back.
6.	B	Answer choice B is correct. The context of "leading to injuries" helps reader understand not to push too hard; hence, utilize.
7.	A	Answer choice A is correct. The word is used in the context of an injury which talks about what it can do to hurt training; therefore, the context indicates the word means "delay".
8.	C	Answer choice C is correct. Stretching loosens things; therefore, the context indicates "limber" means loose.
9.	A	Answer choice A is correct. The definition is given following the word's use.
10.	B	Answer choice B is correct. A dictionary is the right choice.

Lesson 16: Interpreting Figures of Speech (L.8.5.A)

Question	Answer	Detailed Explanation
1.	B	Answer choice B is correct. Like a simile, a metaphor compares two unlike things; however, it does not use like or as in the comparison. Instead, it just makes the statement. For example: The treacherous road snaked wildly through the canyons. In this sentence, the curves of a dangerous (treacherous) road are being compared to the curves of a snake as it slithers across the ground. You could make this sentence say something similar by using a simile instead of a metaphor: The treacherous road curved like a snake through the canyons. Answer choices A, C, and D are incorrect.
2.	C	Answer choice C is correct. Alliteration is the repetition of same letter sounds at the beginning of words or stressed syllables. Onomatopoeia is a sound word like splash, squirt, and plop. Both figures of speech have to do with the sounds of words. Answer choices A, B, and D are incorrect.
3.	C	Answer choice C is correct. Remember a metaphor is like a simile, but doesn't use "like" or "as" in the comparison. In this metaphor, the speaker is comparing his blurry thinking to fog. Answer choice A is a simile. Answer choice B is alliteration. Answer choice D is onomatopoeia.
4.	B	Answer choice B is correct. The phrase "burning the candle at both ends" is an idiom that means a person is doing too much and not getting enough rest, which will eventually exhaust them. If you were to burn a candle at both ends, it would burn out much more quickly than if you had burned it from one end. Answer choices A, C, and D are incorrect.
5.	A	Answer choice A is correct. A fire is bright and diamonds sparkle in the light. Answer choices B, C, and D are incorrect.
6.	B	Answer choice B is correct. This sentence uses a simile to compare the speaker's brother to a machine. Because of the simile, the reader can determine the brother hit the ball flawlessly, like a machine designed to hit balls would. Answer choices A, C, and D are incorrect.
7.	D	Answer choice D is correct. Lions are thought to be courageous, so someone with a lion's heart is courageous. Answer choices A, B, and C are incorrect.
8.	A	Answer choice A is correct. The ability to dance is a human characteristic; therefore, the leaves dancing are an example of personification. Answer choices B, C, and D are incorrect.
9.	B	Answer choice B is correct. When someone sells himself or herself short, he/she is not giving himself/herself enough credit for an accomplishment. Answer choices A, C, and D are incorrect.
10.	B	Answer choice B is correct. I saw the coolest concert last night uses alliteration. Coolest and concert both have the same beginning consonant sound giving the sentence more interest. Answer choices A, C, and D are incorrect.

© Lumos Information Services 2016 | LumosLearning.com

Lesson 17: Relationships Between Words (L.8.5.B)

Question	Answer	Detailed Explanation
1.	B	Answer choice B is correct. An analogy compares two words, specifically two words which can somehow be compared. For example, a heart and a pump. Answer choices A, C, and D are incorrect.
2.	C	Answer choice C is correct. This analogy is comparing a part of a tree (branch) to the whole tree. The second half of the analogy compares part of a hand (fingers) to the whole hand. Answer choices A, B, and D are incorrect.
3.	A	Answer choice A is correct. The first set of words in the analogy are antonyms, repel and attract are opposite in meaning. Therefore, the second half of the analogy should also have a word set which are antonyms. "Follow" is an antonym to "lead". Answer choices B, C and D are not antonyms to the word lead, therefore are incorrect.
4.	B	Answer choice B is correct. Mine is the possessive case of I. The second set in the analogy must, therefore, be the possessive case of "they" which is "theirs". Answer choices A, C, and D are incorrect. Answer choices C and D are not even words.
5.	C	Answer choice C is correct. The first set of words in the analogy, "ostracism" and "acceptance", are antonyms; therefore, the second set of words must also be antonyms. The only antonym to "charitable" is "greedy". Answer choices A, B, and D are incorrect.
6.	C	Answer choice C is correct. The word pairs are homophones meaning each pair sounds the same but are spelled differently and have different meanings. Answer choices A, B, and D are incorrect.
7.	B	Answer choice B is correct. The analogy includes pairs of words are singular and plural. Answer choices A, C, and D are incorrect.
8.	C	Answer choice C is correct. "Tiny" and "small" are synonyms so the word pair must also be synonyms. While "enormous" and "monstrous" could be considered synonyms, the word "large" is a better choice. You must look more at the analogy and notice that the first words in the pair are antonyms: "tiny" and "enormous". Keeping that in mind, the best antonym pair for the second set of words is "small" and "large". Answer choices A and D are incorrect.

Question	Answer	Detailed Explanation
9.	A	Answer choice A is correct. In looking at the analogy, students must first look at the relationship of the word pair and then look at the part of speech. In this case, people watch a television, so it stands to reason that the missing word should be something that people listen to. Students must be very careful, though, to select the matching part of speech - a noun in this case. A radio is a noun and one does listen to a radio. Answer choices B, C, and D are incorrect.
10.	B	Answer choice B is correct. A female adult is a woman, and a female child is a girl. The same relationship must be completed in the analogy. A male adult is a man and a male child is a boy. Answer choices A, C, and D are incorrect.

© Lumos Information Services 2016 | LumosLearning.com

Lesson 18: Denotations and Connotations (L.8.5.C)

Question	Answer	Detailed Explanation
1.	B	Answer choice B is correct. This word is used connotatively to describe that the girl doesn't act her age. Immature is a word in which the connotation can vary depending on the words around it. If it were used to describe a very young child, the connotation would be neutral as young children are immature, or the opposite of mature. In this sentence, immature is used to convey a negative idea. Answer choices A and C are incorrect.
2.	C	Answer choice C is correct. While none of the words have a negative connotation, home conveys to the reader a place where a family lives and is loved. Answer choices A, B, and D have neutral connotations.
3.	A	Answer choice A is correct. In this case, all three words are adjectives used to describe the spending habits of an individual. Being described as cheap has a negative connotation. If you are frugal or thrifty, that means you are careful with your money.
4.	A	Answer choice A is correct. All of the words are adjectives describing something. Plain has the most positive connotation of these words. Dull, ugly, and unattractive all have negative connotations.
5.	A	Answer choice A is correct. Depending upon the text surrounding the word "assertive," the connotation can change. Pushy and aggressive could also be considered somewhat neutral depending upon the surrounding text, but they are generally considered negative.
6.	A	Answer choice A is correct. The word "absurd" is a synonym for funny, but means something unreasonably funny. Answer choices B, C, and D are incorrect because they are all words with positive connotations.
7.	C	Answer choice C is correct. The word "hasty" is used when a decision is made quickly without much thought. Answer choices A, B, and D are incorrect because they are words with positive connotations.
8.	A	Answer choice A is correct. The word "short" has a neutral connotation and generally stays neutral within surrounding text. Answer choices B, C, and D all carry negative connotations.
9.	A	Answer choice A is correct. As used in the sentence, the word "screamed" has a positive connotation. The narrator's mom was happy she won first place and, as a result, her scream was happy.
10.	B	Answer choice B is correct. The narrator's mom was falling from a ladder, something bad that can result in injury. Her scream was from fear; therefore, the connotation is negative.

© Lumos Information Services 2016 | LumosLearning.com

Lesson 19: Domain Specific Words (L.8.6)

Question	Answer	Detailed Explanation
1.	B	Answer choice B is correct. Jargon is words that are specific to an area of study.
2.	D	Answer choice D is correct. All of the examples are specific to literature.
3.	A	Answer choice A is correct. A symbol is specific to literature; therefore, it is domain specific.
4.	C	Answer C is the correct answer. The context clues in the sentence "increased his anxiety" shows that he was frustrated, not angry, annoyed or mad.
5.	A	Answer choice A is correct. Instincts are specific to animals so it is domain specific.
6.	C	Answer choice C is correct. A calculation is specific to math; therefore, it is domain specific.
7.	D	Answer choice D is correct. All of the choices relate to economics; therefore, they are all domain specific.
8.	B	Answer choice B is correct. Meter is specific to poetry; therefore, it is domain specific.
9.	A	Answer choice A is correct. Plugs are specific to cars; therefore, it is domain specific.
10.	A	Answer choice A is correct. A motherboard is specific to a computer; therefore, it is domain specific.

© Lumos Information Services 2016 | LumosLearning.com

Frequently Asked Questions (FAQs)

LEAP FAQs

What will LEAP Assessment Look Like?

In many ways, the LEAP assessments will be unlike anything many students have ever seen. The tests will be conducted online, requiring students complete tasks to assess a deeper understanding of the Louisiana Student Standards. The students will take the Summative Assessment at the end of the year.

The time for the ELA Summative assessment for each grade is given below:

Estimated Time on Task in Minutes			
Grade	Session 1	Session 2	Session 3
3	75	75	60
4	90	75	75
5	90	75	75
6	90	75	75
7	90	75	75
8	90	75	75

How is this Lumos tedBook aligned to LEAP Guidelines?

The practice tests provided in the Lumos Program were created to reflect the depth and rigor of the LEAP assessments based on the information published by the test administrator. However, the content and format of the LEAP assessment that is officially administered to the students could be different compared to these practice tests. You can get more information about this test by visiting www. louisianabelieves.com.

What item types are included in the Online LEAP Test?

Because the assessment is online, the test will consist of a combination of new types of questions:

1. Drag and Drop
2. Evidence Based Selected Response (EBSR)
3. Extended Constructed Response
4. Hot Text Selective Highlight

© Lumos Information Services 2016 | LumosLearning.com

5. Multiple Choice – Single Correct Response, radial buttons
6. Multiple Choice – Multiple Response, check boxes
7. Numeric Response

1. Drag and Drop

This style of question requires the student to move the correct answer from the answer choices into a box. Usually, this box is below the answer choices. If there is more than one box, click on the answer and drag it to the correct box. Hold the answer until it reaches the box and then release the mouse. Often, with multiple boxes, the student may need to continue holding and dragging down as the page scrolls to the correct box.

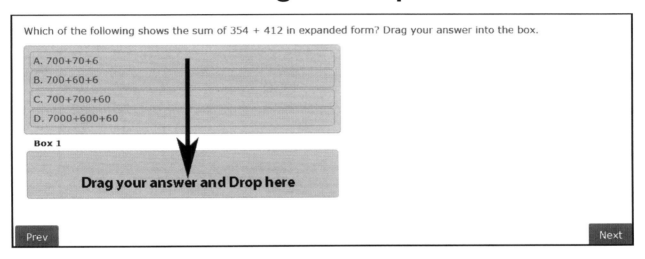

Drag and Drop

Which of the following shows the sum of 354 + 412 in expanded form? Drag your answer into the box.

A. 700+70+6

B. 700+60+6

C. 700+700+60

D. 7000+600+60

Box 1

Drag your answer and Drop here

Prev   Next

2.   Evidence Based Selected Response (EBSR)

- EBSR questions come in 2 parts - PART A and B.
- Both PART A and B could be multiple choice or Part A could be multiple choice while Part B could be some other type.
- Generally, Part A and B will be related, sometimes it may just be from the same lesson but not related questions.
- If it is a Multiple choice question, Select the bubble corresponding to your answer choice.
- Read all of the answer choices, even if think you have found the correct answer.
- In case the questions in EBSR are not multiple choice questions, follow the instruction for other question types while answering such questions.

© Lumos Information Services 2016 | LumosLearning.com

Evidence based selected response

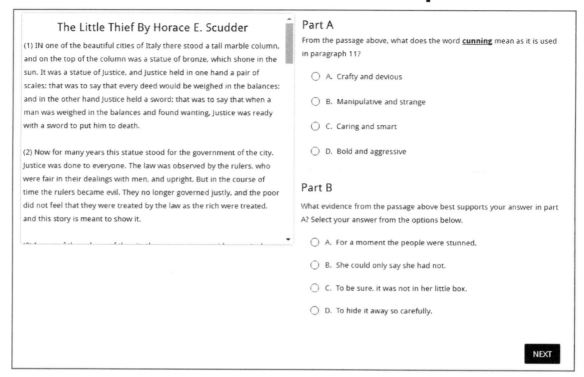

The Little Thief By Horace E. Scudder

(1) IN one of the beautiful cities of Italy there stood a tall marble column, and on the top of the column was a statue of bronze, which shone in the sun. It was a statue of Justice, and Justice held in one hand a pair of scales; that was to say that every deed would be weighed in the balances; and in the other hand Justice held a sword; that was to say that when a man was weighed in the balances and found wanting, Justice was ready with a sword to put him to death.

(2) Now for many years this statue stood for the government of the city. Justice was done to everyone. The law was observed by the rulers, who were fair in their dealings with men, and upright. But in the course of time the rulers became evil. They no longer governed justly, and the poor did not feel that they were treated by the law as the rich were treated. and this story is meant to show it.

Part A

From the passage above, what does the word **cunning** mean as it is used in paragraph 11?

○ A. Crafty and devious

○ B. Manipulative and strange

○ C. Caring and smart

○ D. Bold and aggressive

Part B

What evidence from the passage above best supports your answer in part A? Select your answer from the options below.

○ A. For a moment the people were stunned.

○ B. She could only say she had not.

○ C. To be sure, it was not in her little box.

○ D. To hide it away so carefully.

NEXT

3.   Extended Constructed Response

Similar to Essay Response, the ECR allows students to write their responses to the question. These answers are not as long as essay responses but they are usually longer than just one or two words.

Extended Constructed Response

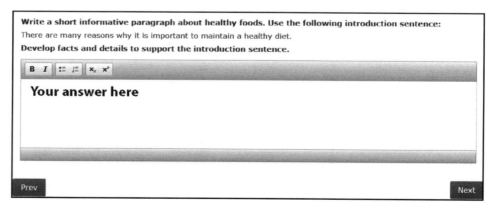

Write a short informative paragraph about healthy foods. Use the following introduction sentence:
There are many reasons why it is important to maintain a healthy diet.
Develop facts and details to support the introduction sentence.

B *I* ≔ ≟ x₀ x²

Your answer here

Prev   Next

© Lumos Information Services 2016 | LumosLearning.com

4. Hot Text Selective Highlight

Hot Text – Selective Highlight asks students to select certain words or phrases from the paragraph for their answer. Often, this type of question will be used when students are asked for supporting information to defend an answer.

Hot Text - Selective Highlight

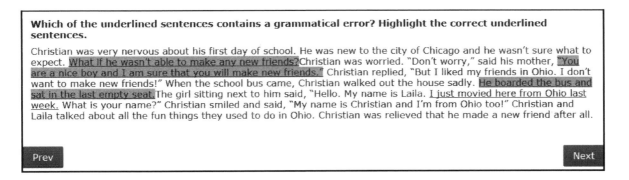

5. Multiple Choice, Single Answer

This style of question is most similar to what students might recognize. It is a standard multiple choice with one answer.

Multiple Choice - Single Response

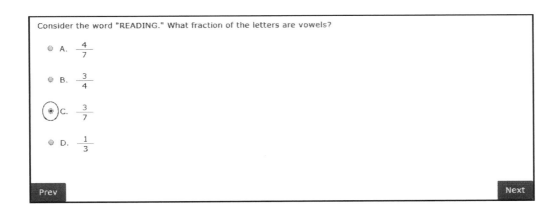

© Lumos Information Services 2016 | LumosLearning.com

6.   Multiple Choice, Multiple Answer

Similar to the previous style, this question asks students to make a selection from options below. However, with the MCMA question, students will need to choose more than one answer. Careful reading of the question is required as it may offer guidance to the number of answer that need to be selected.

Multiple Choice - Multiple Answer

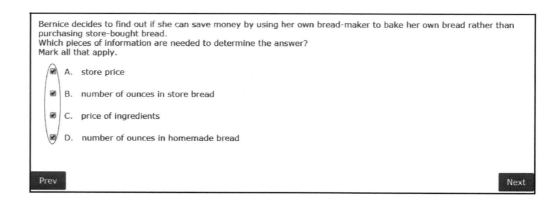

Bernice decides to find out if she can save money by using her own bread-maker to bake her own bread rather than purchasing store-bought bread.
Which pieces of information are needed to determine the answer?
Mark all that apply.

- ☑ A.   store price
- ☑ B.   number of ounces in store bread
- ☑ C.   price of ingredients
- ☑ D.   number of ounces in homemade bread

Prev   Next

7.   Numeric Response

Numeric response questions have a small box where students can type in their solution to a problem. They might use numbers, words, or any combination of both. The question will typically offer guidance to what will go in the box.

Numeric Response

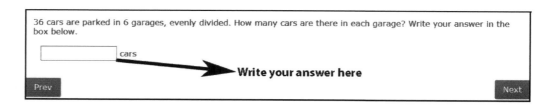

36 cars are parked in 6 garages, evenly divided. How many cars are there in each garage? Write your answer in the box below.

[   ] cars

Write your answer here

Prev   Next

How is this Lumos tedBook aligned to LEAP Guidelines?

The LEAP practice tests offered online at Lumos Learning have been created to accurately reflect the depth and rigor of LEAP. Students will still be exposed to the technology enhanced questions so that they become familiar with the language and practice how to think through these types of tasks.

© Lumos Information Services 2016 | LumosLearning.com

Why Practice with Repeated Reading Passages?

Throughout the Lumos Learning Practice workbooks, students and educators will notice many passages repeat. This is done intentionally. The goal of these workbooks is to help students practice skills necessary to be successful in class and on standardized tests. One of the most critical components to that success is the ability to read and comprehend passages. To that end, reading fluency must be strengthened. According to Hasbrouck and Tindal (2006), "Helping our students become fluent readers is absolutely critical for proficient and motivated reading" (p. 642). And, Nichols et al. indicate, (2009), "fluency is a gateway to comprehension that enables students to move from being word decoders to passage comprehenders" (p. 11).

Lumos Learning recognizes there is no one-size-fits-all approach to build fluency in readers; however, the repeated reading of passages, where students read the same passages at least two or more times, is one of the most widely recognized strategies to improve fluency (Nichols et al., 2009). Repeated reading allows students the opportunity to read passages with familiar words several times until the passage becomes familiar and they no longer have to decode word by word. As students reread, the decoding barrier falls away allowing for an increase in reading comprehension.

The goal of the Lumos Learning workbooks is to increase student achievement and preparation for any standardized test. Using some passages multiple times in a book offers struggling readers an opportunity to do just that.

References
Hasbrouck, J., and Tindal, G. (2006). Oral reading fluency norms: A valuable assessment tool for reading teachers. Reading Teacher, 59(7), 636644. doi:10.1598/RT.59.7.3. Nichols, W., Rupley, W., and Rasinski, T. (2009). Fluency in learning to read for meaning: going beyond repeated readings. Literacy Research & Instruction, 48(1). doi:10.1080/19388070802161906.

© Lumos Information Services 2016 | LumosLearning.com

Lumos StepUp® Mobile App FAQ For Students

What is the Lumos StepUp® App?

It is a FREE application you can download onto your Android smart phones, tablets, iPhones, and iPads.

What are the Benefits of the StepUp® App?

This mobile application gives convenient access to Practice Tests, Common Core State Standards, Online Workbooks, and learning resources through your smart phone and tablet computers.

- Eleven Technology enhanced question types in both MATH and ELA
- Sample questions for arithmetic drills
- Standard specific sample questions
- Instant access to the Common Core State Standards
- Jokes and cartoons to make learning fun!

Do I Need the StepUp® App to Access Online Workbooks?

No, you can access Lumos StepUp® Online Workbooks through a personal computer. The StepUp® app simply enhances your learning experience and allows you to conveniently access StepUp® Online Workbooks and additional resources through your smart phone or tablet.

How can I Download the App?

Visit **lumoslearning.com/a/stepup-app** using your smart phone or tablet and follow the instructions to download the app.

QR Code
for Smart Phone
Or Tablet Users

© Lumos Information Services 2016 | LumosLearning.com

Lumos SchoolUp™ Mobile App FAQ For Parents and Teachers

What is the Lumos SchoolUp™ App?

It is a free app that teachers can use to easily access real-time student activity information as well as assign learning resources to students. Parents can also use it to easily access school-related information such as homework assigned by teachers and information from PTA meetings. It can be downloaded onto smart phones and tablets from popular App Stores.

What are the Benefits of the Lumos SchoolUp™ App?

It provides convenient access to

- Standards aligned learning resources for your students
- An easy to use dashboard
- Student progress reports
- Active and inactive students in your classroom
- Professional development information
- Educational Blogs

How can I Download the App?

Visit **lumoslearning.com/a/schoolup-app** using your smartphone or tablet and follow the instructions provided to download the App. Alternatively, scan the QR Code provided below using your smartphone or tablet computer.

**QR Code
for Smart Phone
Or Tablet Users**

© Lumos Information Services 2016 | LumosLearning.com

Lumos StepUp® Teacher Portal FAQ

The Lumos Learning Teacher Portal gives teachers insights into their students' work and access to useful resources.

Student Reports

The 'Student Report' tab is the heart of the teacher portal. It is where teachers can create their student accounts, gather information about their list of students, class performance, individual student performance, and explore the list of subscribed content.

Progress Summary

This allows teachers to follow the progress of each of their students. From here, teachers can see overall progress of each student. They can then click on a specific student's name and see the individual details of progress. Additionally, teachers, can click on questions to be graded (essays and constructed responses for example).

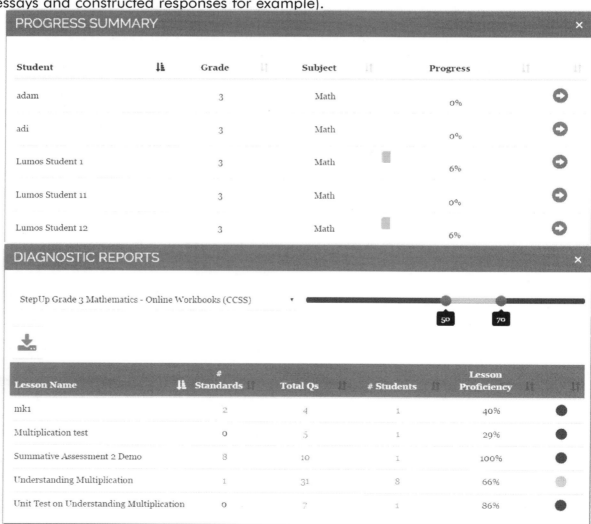

© Lumos Information Services 2016 | LumosLearning.com

My Lessons

This allows teachers to see all content to which they have subscribed. From this the teachers can assign specific work to their students. A teacher can assign an individual lesson to the student through the 'Custom Assessments' link; from there, the teacher can select from the list of lessons available. Students will then receive an alert about the assigned lesson.

My Students

This tab allows teachers to see all login information for their assigned students. They can change passwords and create student accounts in this tab.

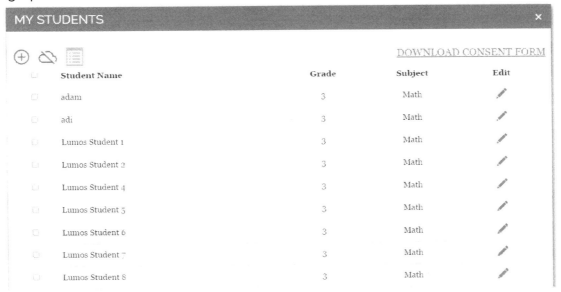

© Lumos Information Services 2016 | LumosLearning.com

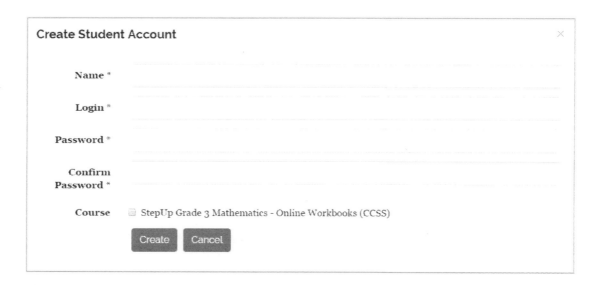

Insights

The insights tab is one of the most powerful components of the teacher portal. It allows teachers to gain a deeper understanding of how their students are progressing. Individualized reports can be generated for specific date ranges. Student performance data can be categorized into partial, proficient, and advanced sections. Additionally, teachers can customize what guidelines they would like to use for not meeting the standard (low bar), meeting the standard, and achieving above the standard. This report can be used to drive instruction and practice and identify the topics where students might need additional assistance in to master the standard.

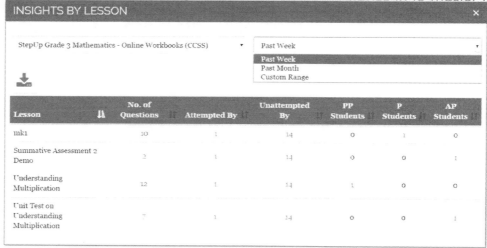

© Lumos Information Services 2016 | LumosLearning.com

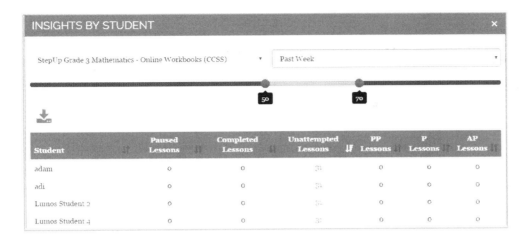

Stickies

Stickies are an exciting new way to share any type of school related information with parents and students.

- Need to share your school supply list?
- Have a great resource to exchange with others?
- Want to ensure parents can see a copy of the homework?
- Want to recommend a mobile app?
- Want to suggest a book?

Create a Stickie!

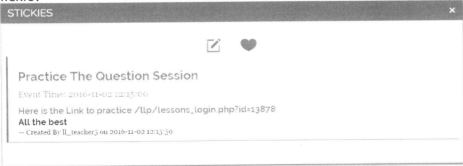

© Lumos Information Services 2016 | LumosLearning.com

Ed Blogs

Lumos Learning teachers consistently monitor current educational trends and topics. Exploring the EdBlogs tab allows teachers to follow the blogs and stay current on important educational topics.

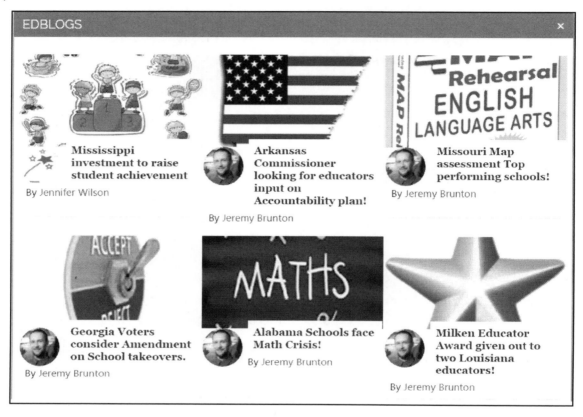

© Lumos Information Services 2016 | LumosLearning.com

EdSearch

EdSearch is a comprehensive directory for educational resources and organizations. Using the search box, discover hundreds of standard aligned educational books, apps, and videos. Get ready access to thousands of grade appropriate practice questions and lessons. Find nearby schools, libraries, school supply stores, conferences and more. View school test scores, enrollments, calendar events and much more. Compare school ratings and ranking.

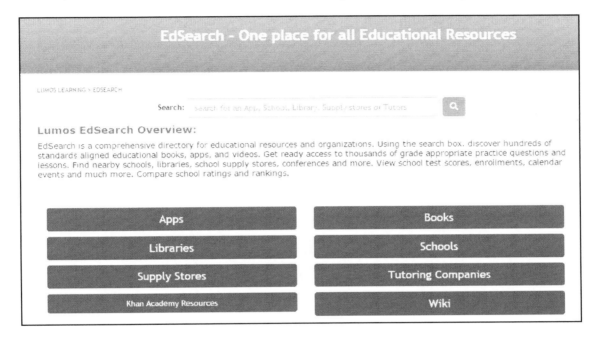

© Lumos Information Services 2016 | LumosLearning.com

Lumos Learning
Developed by Expert Teachers

Grade **8**

LEAP Math Practice

((tedBook))

ONLINE

Two Practice Tests

7 Tech-Enhanced Item Types

30+ SKILLS

www.LumosLearning.com

LEAP is a registered trademark of Louisiana Department of Education, which does not sponsor or endorse this product.

Available

- At Leading book stores
- Online www.LumosLearning.com

78308268R00129

Made in the USA
Columbia, SC
15 October 2017